BIBLE PARENTS

BIBLE PARENTS

TRAVAIL AND TRIUMPH

JAMES KIFER

NEW HARBOR PRESS

RAPID CITY, SD

Kifer/New Harbor Press
1601 Mt. Rushmore Rd., Ste 3228
Rapid City, SD 57701
www.newharborpress.com

Ordering Information:
Quantity sales. Special discounts are available on quantity purchases by corporations, associations, and others. For details, contact the "Special Sales Department" at the address above.

Bible Parents/Kifer. -- 1st ed.
ISBN 978-1-63357-162-4

CONTENTS

Preface

 I have never read a book or even a single magazine article devoted to the subject of parenthood. This omission is due neither to a lack of interest or of experience, for I became a parent at the age of twenty-four and am now the father of two beautiful daughters. Over four decades of fatherhood has altered, modified and shifted some of my earlier views on this vital subject, but I believe the central determining principles to which I aspired then remain essentially the same today. This is only natural as time and events are continuous evolutionary forces in life, and they constantly change, erode and even polish earlier confirmed beliefs we cherish.

It is natural, fundamental and axiomatic that we expect and anticipate that children will grow from infancy to mature adulthood. As much as we delight in a baby's cuteness and innocence its other qualities of endless time demands and unmitigated selfishness are more difficult to tolerate and in fact are abhorrent in an adult. The natural progression of any person from infancy to adulthood reflects the transience of the many phases of development. Likewise, this is true (or should be so) with the parents of that child. It is often, if not generally, overlooked that parents develop through phases just as do their children. As the newborn changes to the toddler, the child, the adolescent teenager to the young vibrant adult and finally to the mature and senior adult each parent travels a similar timeline. The concepts, ideas and ideals that are cherished and held so firmly upon the first child's birth are often altered or even supplanted by others through many years of experience, troubles and joy. What the young man or woman envisions before initiation into parenthood and clings to rigidly and rigorously through the early years of parenthood is seen as a citadel of virtue, knowledge and wisdom. Yet that citadel is often eroded, even corroded by the winds and storms of raising the child. In fact, this citadel may even be beleaguered and breached by the passing years of parental problems. Not by experience alone, whether bad or good, does the parent grow, but also by the slow accretion of the mother or father's own knowledge and wisdom. What is crystal clear in the early years often finds itself shadowed by the cruel logic of factual development, and these matters give rise in the parent's mind not to new and fresh certainties but rather to hesitation, questioning and parental self-doubt.

So, what does someone such as myself have to offer to the great, unending conversation of how to raise children and then later relate to them as fellow adults? Admittedly I possess neither a scholastic background in the subject and no particular personal interest in the ongoing discussion of the contemporary parental scene. Should I attempt to offer my own experience as a guideline I would rightly be convicted of egotism and hubris. On this as on most subjects a person's own experiences are generally interesting only to himself and perhaps a few close family members. What this compilation of essays offers is not myself, and neither does it promise anything new, for as the proverbial expression of old was rendered "...there is nothing new under the sun."

The contribution of this work to the compendium and turbulence of parental discussions, in fact, a book, the suggestion of which creates a paradox, for this is a contradiction to the first statement of this preface. Regarding existing "parental" literature I make no generalized statement of either praise or denigration. Undoubtedly the modern library contains many well-written, thoughtful and stimulating works on the subject at hand. It is just as likely to offer many slipshod and superfluous volumes that often have only a tenuous connection to reality. So, is the arena of parental advice now left solely to the descent of the accumulated wisdom of our forebears and our own experiences? Although these sources are quite valuable and in no degree to be the subject of mocking one other source remains as a mine of wisdom and stories, of instruction, guidance, triumphs and no shortage even of parental failures. That source is the oldest source of all, the most praised, the most derided, the most studied, the most ignored, but still standing. It is the Bible.

One quick and anticipated reaction to the above statement is a rejoinder of "Not so!" The Bible, you say, is often cited as a parents' guidebook, followed more closely and reverently by our ancestors then us, yet followed nonetheless. In part this is a logical and correct response for the Bible has become a book of quotations and maxims to which parents should faithfully adhere, filled with admonitions such as:

"Spare the rod and spoil the child."

"Train up a child in the way should go: and
when he is old will not depart from it."

As a source of axiomatic statements and words of wisdom the scriptures ever remain a singular source of wisdom. These and many other proverbial sayings glow with a radiance and wisdom which is surpassed only by the statements of Christ Himself. Often overlooked or downplayed, though a treasure trove of lessons that provide the structural foundation and spine of the Old Testament. The importance of these narratives is continued and is emphasized by the commencement of the New Testament with the most famous parent-child relationship of all, Mary and Joseph as mother and father in the nativity of Jesus.

An analysis of the Bible's initial book of Genesis reveals that after the first few chapters it is essentially the story of one family, a family upon which the Biblical and historical spotlight began to shine when God called out its patriarch, Abraham, from his home in the Chaldees. From that momentous event flows a river of stories that have long been the heart and soul of Biblical teaching, Abraham, Sarah and Isaac to Isaac, Rebekah and their sons Jacob and Esau and the children of Jacob. The narrative tale of each is centered around the parent/child relationship. Another family is called centuries later as the wise old prophet Samuel, anoints the young David as King. What follows from God's decision there sets the historical fate and destiny for all Israel and the spiritual destiny of all humanity.

As historically and scripturally as are all these epic stories, a human element contained in each is often ignored or relegated to children's Sunday School lessons. Every story, no matter how historically grand it may be, is also a gripping account of a parent(s) interaction with sons and daughters. At times the decisions and actions of parents are wise, loving and even noble, and at other points foolish, short sighted and even deplorable. Yet no matter how long ago they were made and acted the stories retain the relevance of the moment because they illustrate so vividly timeless principles of parenthood.

As great and sweeping is the grandeur of many of the Old Testament stories of parenthood they remain in the shadow of the figure and the teaching of a man who himself was never a parent, Jesus Christ. His own life was the model of everything, including Sonship, and the "ordinary" persons whom He encountered and the short powerful lessons He taught remain the touchstone and the embodiment of the ideal of parenthood.

A permeating theme of these essays is the frequency of which so called ordinary decisions would have lasting historical effects far beyond the generations in which these persons actually lived. For example, the decisions made by Rebekah and Isaac to show favoritism to Jacob and Esau respectively effectively destroyed their original family, set the course of Hebrew history for centuries and in a very tangible way was a mechanism through which God changed His relationship with mankind, a change that is yet effective.

The father of eight sons, a man named Jesse, decided that the youngest would be assigned the lonely and menial duties of a shepherd. The stream of consequences which flowed from that choice grew ever wider and has not yet been fully spent. In the New Testament especially the components of family life are examined, and we see that the mother and father of first century Judea lived with the same parental questions, worries, melancholy, grief and joy as we do now. The patient, aggrieved, taken for granted father in the parable of the prodigal son experiences heartache, loss, fear, anticipation, joy, elation and the bitterness of one son. How common is that to any parent in any century? The horror and pain of watching a beloved child slowly slip into the cold clutches of death is the fate of Jairus. The most famous and honored mother in history, Mary, the mother of Jesus, has bestowed upon her the overwhelming honor of giving birth to the Son of God and the joys and wonders of seeing Him grow in favor and stature from infancy to mature adulthood. Yet in the greatest definition and expression ever of "bittersweet" she is forewarned that "...a sword shall pierce through thy own soul" as she witnessed and maternally partook of her Son's persecution and passion.

The Holy Bible is a storehouse, a cornucopia of so many things, but one hesitates to call it a parents' manual in any sense. The prevailing culture and ethic for modern parenting seems to stress and emphasize the years of childhood and adolescence. This itself is commendable, for these are the times in which basic character is almost always shaped and fashioned. These are the days when the basic traits of a man or a woman are more easily malleable when they are in the persons of a boy or girl. Study reflects, though, that most Biblical stories and lessons and most of the teachings and moral are discovered in histories and parables of parents and their adult children.

While the Bible is in no way devoid of narratives in which children are characters it is by no means a centerpiece of Biblical teachings.

No observing person needs to have read a library of parental literature or even to be a parent to realize and comprehend the current cultural milieu and ethic regarding this vital subject. No doubt this is once again an expression of Divine wisdom. For all the romanticism and sentimentalism, our joy and longing for the idealized halcyon days of childhood most of our lives are spent in the adult world. Yet, in a very real sense we remain children to our parents, even after those mothers and fathers have passed from this world. It is from this world, this source, that the Bible offers most of its stories regarding parenthood, and it is from here the relevancy of its teachings is found. The Bible, even by its Christian adherents is often utilized to justify parental attitudes, actions and policies by a quote or two from its pages. Sometimes the principle of child obedience is stressed, almost to the exclusion of any other principles. This is the parental philosophy that finds its simplest expression in the statement "Do it because I said so." While all exasperated parents have resorted to this it hardly suffices as the cornerstone of parenting and in fact in its purest sense is non-Biblical.

Swinging the pendulum to the other extreme is the modern (or perhaps post-modern) philosophy of endless therapy, counseling, rewards, praise, permissiveness, etc. All these factors have a place in parenting, yet as with authoritarian directives alone from parents to children they fail when they are employed as the entirety of parenting. This philosophy of parenting has no moral anchor, and in reality, is blown about by the trending, prevalent winds of the moment.

An old adage expressed in various forms but nowhere issued better than "I would rather see a sermon than hear one" may be mocked and scorned, but it contains the bedrock of truth. Among so many other lessons the Bible is a book of living sermons on parenting. Yes, they are all stories of persons who are temporal and have long since left this world, but their realism and relevance are easily and quickly seen. These are sermons of good, even great parents, inconsistent parents, distracted parents and in one instance brought forth here horrible parents. In other words, though, they lived in millennia past, dressed differently, spoke different languages, held different trades and occupations they are us. Their lives, stories, triumphs and failures as parents deserve a brighter spotlight than is now shined upon them. Hopefully their lives as unwitting examples and teachers have greater illumination because of this small work.

Personally, I have been blessed beyond adequate expression in my walk as a father. My fellow parent, Debbie, my wife and the mother of Jennifer and Gretchen, has been the exemplar of motherhood and possesses a character and spirit the equal of any woman in either the Old or New Testaments. Long ago the earthly bonds between my own mother and father were broken when they passed from this temporal sphere. Yet, their character and personality, their words and actions and my memories linger still. Always, wherever I have been and wherever I go they abide with me, for by their example I learned the meaning of Micah 6:8. To these three, my beloved wife and parents I dedicate the few thoughts of this book.

Chapter 1

THE EPIC OF ABRAHAM

So much began in a locale with the strange and almost mystical name of Ur of the Chaldees. Here, close to the Tigris and Euphrates rivers in what is now Iraq lived a man named Terah in this, his native land. Our knowledge of Terah is relegated to this one simple, stark fact except for other minor scraps of information the Book of Genesis reveals. Terah was the father of three sons, the first named of which was Abram. Upon Terah's death Abram was given a Divine commission to...

> "Get thee out of thy country, and from thy kindred,
> and from thy father's house, unto a land I will show
> thee: And I will make of thee a great nation...:

So, Abram (later to be renamed Abraham by God) gathered his property and along with his wife, Sarai, "went forth into the land of Canaan," later to be known by a plethora of names, Palestine, Judah, Judea, and finally Israel. Abraham's obedient move to Canaan has proven to be a wellspring for many things, the effects of which still bear an enormous influence thousands of years later in our present twenty-first century. Inarguably is the establishment of the lineage from which would come Jesus Christ and salvation. God also promised to Abraham that His blessings would include a multiplication of Abraham's descendants so that they would be "...as the stars of the heaven, and the sand which is upon the sea shore." True to His word God made Abraham the progenitor of the Semitic peoples, from the Arabs to the most noteworthy of the Semites, the Jewish people. In a very literal, very real sense the remainder of the Old and all the New Testament is the story of Abraham's descendants. The nation of Israel itself was founded by the lineage of Abraham's seed, through his grandson Jacob and twelve great grandsons.

All of this is quite familiar and even second nature to any person with a reasonably good knowledge of the scriptures. Yet Abraham was more than a historical figure, more than a religious vessel or icon through which God worked His will. He was the first patriarch and the founder of a family composed of the same elements as the modern family. Obviously, parents and their children were present and comprised the many generations before Abraham and Sarah, but it is they around whom the Biblical narrative swirls and finally focuses. Denied their desire of children early in their marriage, a frustrated Abraham turned away from Sarah and his first son was borne by the young woman Hagar (servant to Sarah and with Sarah's full knowledge and complicity). This boy's name was Ishmael, who would become progenitor of a large compendium of Semitic nationalities, a full list of which would be exhaustive. A long list, but one which did not include the chosen seed, those people known by many names, first Hebrews, Israelites and now most commonly Jews. The promised child would come through Abraham's aged wife Sarah, and his name was Isaac.

Deferring for a bit the father/son relationship of Abraham and Isaac, we come upon Isaac as a grown man. In accordance with ancient custom, his father Abraham assumes the role of securing a bride for Isaac. Abraham dispatches his steward to Mesopotamia (Abraham's original land) and finds a fair young beauty named Rebekah. With the ancient authority granted the steward, he betroths Rebekah to Isaac, a betrothal that pre-dates her meeting

Isaac or any of his family. Though shocking this ancient custom may be to the modern sensibility, in this instance it worked, for the marriage was long and fruitful. Isaac and Rebekah truly loved each other and are exemplary to us in many ways. With the death of his father Abraham, Isaac became the patriarch of his own and his extended family, but as were his parents he was growing older without sons. Isaac's prayerful petitions to God were granted and Rebekah bore him not one, but two sons, names and characters that still forcefully resound to the present, Jacob and Esau.

It would be appealing, inspiring and comforting to speak and write of the superb examples of motherhood and fatherhood that were the lives of Rebekah and Isaac. It certainly would be a warm radiating story, but in a very important fashion one word most describes a large aspect of the parenthood of Isaac and Rebekah. The word is terrible. No, undoubtedly, they were not terrible in the sense that they were cruel, physically or emotionally, to Jacob and Esau. Doubtless they were worthy parents in the matter of adequate care and provision for their sons. Isaac and Rebekah missed the mark in a dangerous, albeit quite common today, manner as parents. Each of them injected into the parent-child relationship a poison so virulent that it became systemic, corrupting and multiplying into many succeeding generations and influencing the course of history, both temporal and spiritual. It was the vile venom of favoritism, for as Genesis famously records:

"And Isaac loved Esau... but Rebekah loved Jacob."

This favoritism was by no means inexplicable for each parent doubtless witnessed a vision of himself or herself in the two twins.

Whether divinely designed or not the two boys had an enmity which pre-dated their births. In the stark, descriptive and at times colorful language of the Old Testament we are told that:

"... the first came out red, all over like a hairy garment; and they called his name Esau.

And after that came his brother out, and his hand
took hold on Esau's heel; and his name was called
Jacob..."

What is both prophesied and here foreshadowed is that the two sons would struggle with the result that "...the elder shall serve the younger." So, began the construction of a stage upon which the long, fascinating and in many ways tragic conflict between the two sons began. Jacob and Esau were twins, fraternal, not identical, and by definition brothers. Life's experiences reflect that some twins are not only identical in looks but also in personality and character, while others to varying degrees are exceptions to this. Jacob and Esau were by birth and inheritance almost polar opposites, as the transience of time and their maturity so demonstrated:

"And the boys grew; and Esau was a cunning
hunter, a man of the field; and Jacob was a plain
man, dwelling in tents"

Such a brotherly dichotomy of interests is certainly neither shocking, uncommon nor surprising. Many are the examples which all can cite of brothers and sisters with varying interests and differing personalities who enjoy the other's company and enrich each other's lives. All but the most rigid social science ideologue would concur that each person is borne with a certain set of personality traits which may be modified but not negated. So, it was with Jacob and Esau, and taken on its own neither was the worse for it, but Jacob and Esau did not live and grow in a vacuum. Again, a very short descriptive sentence fraught with meaning for the two sons, fateful to the entire family's history and hugely determinative of spiritual history reads:

"And Isaac loved Esau, but Rebekah loved Jacob."

As the great story unfolds it is not unfair to say that this truth was the foundation of the parental attitudes and skills of Isaac and

Rebekah. It is also a truth that is as common in families in all dispensations, ages, cultures, climes and situations so is the institution of the family itself. It has been the cruel destroyer of parental/child bonds, sibling relationships and entire family structures, and we know it by its most common and appropriate title – favoritism. Just as deplorable as it may be it can be just as common, and frankly just as explicable.

Loving one son to the detriment or even exclusion of the other is not a truth surrounded by clouds of mystery. Often a parent and child have a special bond due to any number of a large array of traits, common interests, pursuits, personalities or just the special enjoyment of each other's company and presence. Perhaps it will be an undefinable, inexplicable quality which binds the two. Doubtless most parents have felt this pull towards one child during their tenure as parents, and obviously so did Isaac and Rebekah. The bonds which the father enjoyed with Esau and the mother with Jacob was likely based on many factors. Yet the Bible sets forth the plainest of facts, i.e. that the parental bonds were founded upon similarity. As Genesis records, Esau was a "cunning hunter" and "did eat of (Isaac's venison)." Esau was an outdoorsman, a great hunter and in today's parlance "a man's man." Jacob, conversely, was a tent-dweller, a shepherd, and fully possessed of his mother's intelligence and cunning.

By either design, happenstance, negligence or an amalgam of all Rebekah and Isaac had committed a cardinal sin in parenting. They had created two families, Rebekah and Jacob posed against Isaac and Esau. Both "families" effectively would be in calamitous ruin at the end.

One day Esau returned unsuccessfully from one of his regular hunting trips. He was exhausted, weakened, starving, and in his own words "...at the point to die." Fortunately, he happily encountered Jacob, his twin brother, and even more fortuitously Jacob was preparing just what Esau craved, food. Esau's elation was short lived, as the clever and ruthless Jacob knew he possessed the leverage of an undreamt bargaining position. Certainly, related Jacob to his brother, I will share my food with you but only as the part of a greater bargain. "Sell me this day thy birthright..." and your hunger shall be assuaged. Esau, a man who easily played the role of what Christ would later call the "carnal man," shrugged away the moment and the birthright. "What profit shall this birthright do to me?" he exclaimed as he ravenously devoured bread and a pottage of lentils.

No observer should ever lightly brush away the gross and dark character traits of both brothers in this famous narrative. It is appalling that Esau so lightly regards his birthright, the legal claim to the greatest proportion of the family's wealth, for one meal, but Jacob's actions are yet more despicable. What brother or sister would initiate contractual negotiations where a sibling was on the brink of starvation? As with all persons, each brother answers for his own actions, but what did the mother and father do which opened the route to this ghastly scene? All, especially those who are parents, should be reluctant to quickly offer judgments on the conduct of other parents. Still, the blatant favoritism which was shown by both Isaac and Rebekah almost requires us to assign them culpability for this horrid event, and even more surely for a worse tragedy which was to follow.

Isaac was aging and felt (wrongly as it was shown) that he was failing, and death was near. In preparation for this he determined to stage a ceremony at which his son was to receive his father's patriarchal blessing. Although only the elder by the length of a few moments Esau was legitimately entitled to the blessing. His father sent him on a hunting expedition to find the deer and its venison, which Isaac so enjoyed. Esau was to return with the venison whereupon Isaac would dine prior to giving him the blessing.

Such a momentous occasion a sharp-eyed and intelligent observer such as Rebekah could not ignore or allow to pass without her influence. Quickly, she organized and implemented a scheme so devious and so effective that it astounds us still. Age had robbed Isaac of his sight, and Rebekah sought to use this to full advantage. Go to your flock of sheep and goats, she directed Jacob, take two young ones and I will make for your father Isaac the savory stew he so enjoys. After his repast you, Jacob, will enter your father's presence and receive from him the patriarchal blessing to be head of the family. Jacob easily saw the flaw in Rebekah's plan, for although Isaac was blind he retained his other senses. Jacob protested that when Isaac began to give him the blessing he would realize that he was being duped, for the blessing was accompanied by the father's physically embracing his son. Facts remain facts, and so Jacob was aware as he protested to his mother:

> "Behold, Esau, my brother is a hairy man, and I am
> a smooth man: My father will feel me, and I shall
> seem to him as a deceiver; and I shall bring a curse
> upon me, and not a blessing."

Well said, but this fraud was well served by Rebekah. Every criminal conspiracy needs a mastermind, and this enterprise had such a one in Rebekah. Dress in Esau's garments, she instructed Jacob, and then place on your forearms and hands the hairy pelts from the goats we have utilized. This will fool your father, and as for any curse, let it be upon me, Rebekah blithely exclaimed.

How often do the most complex yet well-planned schemes go awry? One misstep, one overlooked detail, one inadvertent word can collapse the entire endeavor. Not this time. The heist of the blessing by Rebekah and Jacob slides down a path of perfection. Although Isaac is startled by Jacob's voice, he nonetheless pronounces the patriarchal blessing upon the younger brother. Jacob scarcely left the presence of his father when the son entitled to the blessing came into the tent of Isaac. Esau's actions were entirely and explicitly correct, and it was only his performance that was inexpedient. Upon Esau's greeting his father, Isaac literally trembled and soon realized that his own son had succeeded exceptionally well in fooling his father. In bitter agony of soul Esau exclaimed that his brother had taken his birthright and had now stolen his blessing. Esau desperately pleaded with Isaac for a second blessing. Not only was he denied the blessing but you "...shalt serve your brother." In shock, disappointment and seething rage Esau turned from his father and to the looming specter of a confrontation with Jacob. Anticipating the likely death of Isaac, Esau deferred the result of his emotions; however, after "the days of mourning for my father..." Esau vowed to kill his brother, now hated by Esau.

Rebekah's matriarchal antenna was keen to all this. Hearing of Esau's oath to destroy Jacob, she advised her beloved younger son to become a fugitive to the land of Haran and there stay with her brother Laban. Wait awhile, she counseled Jacob, until Esau's anger abates, and you may return home. Fearing what would transpire should Jacob abide with them at home, she realized that the murder of Jacob would likewise result in the condemnation of Esau.

"Why should I be deprived also of you
both in one day?"

So, what is now the state of this family, a family that held so much promise? It must have been so easy, even from the beginning, for the two parents to demonstrate partiality and favoritism. Isaac had in Esau not only a strong, virile, manly son, but also a companion and likely in modern terms a friend and playmate as well. They liked the same things, the same ways, and each seemed to revel in the company of the other. Who Rebekah found in Jacob was an exceptionally bright mind, a calm demeanor and a talent for sharp dealing and lying which matched her own. This split of family affections and of parental bonds for children ultimately proved fatal to the family unit. Neither Isaac nor Rebekah ever seemed to grasp that parental love is not a limited quality to be rationed among sons and daughters. By loving Esau and having a special bond with him did not dictate to Isaac that he must love Jacob less, and the same was true for Rebekah and Jacob. Instead this family could boast of two great parent/child bonds and two equally large dysfunctional bonds. By favoring Jacob so blatantly Rebekah not only harmed Esau but ultimately devastated her husband Isaac.

Jacob leaves his home and escapes the murderous wrath of Esau, traveling to Haran and beginning his prophesied role as family patriarch. If anything, the story of his large, instrumental and influential family is packed with more spiritual potency than that of he and his brother Esau. With his uncle Laban he is about to commence a long, arduous and fateful schooling in the arts of chicanery, lying and double dealing. Nonetheless, as will later be seen, God's will ultimately triumphs, but it is a triumph that marches flanked by the companionship of family misery and enmity. Jacob not only survives but prospers and is honored. But what of the parents, Isaac and Rebekah, who are doubtless left wondering of the fate and status of a son? Whatever the status of Rebekah's plans for her beloved Jacob they were fulfilled in an arena far from Rebekah.

In the wake of the theft of his blessing the immediate trajectory of Esau's life was downward. He took to himself two Hittite wives, a flaunting of the law for two reasons. They were outsiders to the Abrahamic clan and were thus idol worshippers. Those hauntingly dark words of Genesis portend an emotion which so many parents sadly recognize, that Esau's conduct was "...a grief of mind unto Isaac and to Rebekah."

Happily, the reconciliation between Esau and Jacob was eventually made later in life when both were wealthy men with large families of their own. The text offers an emotional reunion where Esau forgives Jacob and demonstrates his great growth as a man. Rebekah and Isaac now were quite aged and soon to die and had missed decades of companionship with their sons, grandchildren and all their kin. The Bible supplies no answer to an obvious question. Did Isaac and Rebekah ever realize that by loving one son disproportionately at the expense of another a deadly destructive disease had been introduced? As one greater than all later stated "...a house divided against itself shall not stand."

Chapter 2

JACOB RELIVES THE OLD, OLD STORY

*I*t was a long journey which Jacob was to make from his home in Canaan to the land of Padan-aram (the plains of Syria), a journey that had to be made. Yet geographical measure is not the only standard of length. In the very prime and vigor of life Jacob was charged by his father to abandon Canaan and any dreams of marriage to a Canaanite woman and now go to the home of Laban, Rebekah's brother and make a new life with people who though kin were strangers to Jacob. Abandon the daily love of a doting mother, forsake the successful life of a shepherd and the respect which he had earned and accrued and effectively begin in a new world.

When a child leaves the home of his/her parents so many emotions are companions, and these were doubtless writ large with Jacob. Sadness at leaving the parental hearth and embrace, regret that a stage of life has now ended, and melancholy at leaving the friends and familiar scenes of youth. Also, he is accompanied by the excitement and thrill of a new life, with new friends and new adventures. One emotion, though, surely strides with him every step of the way, and that is a fear for the unknown future. So, did Jacob begin his long journey, and in that sojourn, he discovered that he possessed something else which he had overlooked.

One night while on the trail Jacob made his bed by piling stones and using them as his pillow. When sleep overtook him and likewise did his dreams, he viewed a ladder from earth to heaven with angels ascending and descending upon its steps. And Jacob saw God above it all, a God who now renewed his covenants that He had made with Jacob's grandfather Abraham and father Isaac. Now, it is with you Jacob, said God, and through your lineage shall all the nations of the earth be blessed. As much as mortal man can be aware Jacob knew the momentous import of this moment and vowed that he would walk with the God of his fathers.

This was much more than a spiritual journey, great as it was, for Jacob. He finally reached Haran where he was assured by a familiar sight, flocks of sheep and their shepherds. As comforting as they were the grand sight for Jacob's eyes was the younger daughter of his uncle and soon to be employer. Her name was Rachel, "beautiful and well favored...", and their first meeting at a water well proves that "love at first sight" is more than mythology. Jacob's heart leaped when he saw this young beauty, kissed her and set in motion decades of family and Bible history. An early wedding was not to be, though, for Jacob had met his match and perhaps his superior in the skills of hard bargaining and chicanery, his uncle Laban. In this ancient patriarchal dispensation, the father as the head of the family possessed enormous authority. Laban was elated at his prospective new son-in-law but required seven years of work from Jacob prior to the wedding. So great was Jacob's desire for Rachel that the seven years were as a "few days" earning him the contractual and marital rights to the new bride. The wedding and its accompanying feast were joyous (and likely raucous) occasions, but in the evening Jacob (perhaps a bit inebriated) went in to consummate his love for Rachel. In the morning he awoke and found that he had spent the wedding night in bed with ...Rachel's older sister Leah, she of tender eyes but plain looks.

A furious Jacob confronted Laban, whose lies were hidden in darkness but exposed in light, and now explained that as the younger Rachel could not marry before Leah. The duplicitous uncle, and now father-in-law, saw and ravenously grasped the opportunity to make a good situation for himself even better. Certainly you may have Rachel as another wife, he soothes Jacob, but I must also ask seven years more work from you, my dear son-in-law Jacob. At Laban's demand Jacob tarried seven days more and then was given the desired and beautiful Rachel as his second bride. Jacob's obligation for seven years more labor remained, but he would have the beloved Rachel as a wife during this term. He would also have Leah. Thus, began Biblical history's first "blended" family, and in many ways its most famous to this day.

Blended family is a modern term, a two-word phrase which contains both the catchiness and the clank of much modern phraseology. The players in this mixture include the two wives and Jacob himself, as well as twelve sons and one daughter, all of whom deserve an introduction by name. By Leah Jacob's sons were Reuben, Simeon, Levi, Judah, Naphtali, Asher, Issachar, Zebulun and daughter Dinah. After eleven had been born God favored Rachel with sons Joseph and Benjamin. From handmaids Bilhah and Zillah, Dan and Gad respectively were born. A total of one husband, two wives, two mistresses, twelve sons and one daughter, composed this blended family unit. The trouble, as with many blended families then and now is that they blended not.

From this moment forward the long narrative of Genesis is the story of this family, the love, the hatreds, the jealousies, the self-dealing and lying, and finally a dramatic denouement which is the equal of any human story and the superior of any fiction. Yet for year upon year certain curious consistencies remained with this family. Jacob continued to work for Laban, and Jacob's prosperity as well as his family was ever growing. This polygamous family retained the same two wives, Leah and Rachel, with the latter retaining Jacob's love and favor. None of this passed without the notice of the true patriarch God, whose feelings on the wifely favoritism of Jacob were thus expressed:

> "And when the Lord saw that Leah was hated, he
> opened her womb: but Rachel was barren."

In a time and culture where many women measured their worth by their number of children God's favor to Leah is certainly understood. After Jacob had become the father of ten sons and a daughter, Rachel too was blessed, and she became the mother of Jacob's final two sons, Joseph and Benjamin.

Jacob certainly merited the titles of husband and father, as he had sired a prodigious family by four different women. Still, though, his combat with Laban continued. After a lengthy tenure of matching wits and schemes with his father-in-law he began to remove his family from Haran. Earlier he had come as a sole fugitive from the wrath of brother Esau. Now, twenty years hence, Jacob was the head and patriarch of a large clan of wives, children, servants and huge flocks of sheep, goats and cattle. In trenchant terms, Jacob had become a great man. A great man, but also a man now greatly hated by Laban. Jacob's tenure as Laban's servant included not only years of work but years of conflict and scheming. Jacob, though, had finally gotten the upper hand, the two daughters of Laban and much of Laban's wealth in livestock. His time in Haran was now closing, and God directed him back to Bethel and to his family. After escaping the wrath of Laban, he continued his journey to Bethel at the head of his great family and with a new name of historic consequences now bestowed by God, Israel.

Jacob was not the only great man in the midst of a migration, for he received news that a terrifying specter from his past, perhaps the man he feared the most was coming to meet him, his defrauded brother Esau. But not Esau alone, not just the wild hunter of his youth, but a betrayed brother at the head of an army of four hundred men. Surely, Jacob surmised, Esau was come to seek vengeance and retaliate for the wrongs done him by his brother. Fully anticipating a violent clash Jacob knew that no escape route beckoned and for better or worse Esau must be faced. While Jacob lacked nothing for personal bravery he now resorted to a familiar family trait and engaged in an act of favoritism so gross and grotesque that it is described adequately only by the scriptures:

> "And he divided the children unto Leah, and unto
> Rachel, and unto the two handmaids
> And he put the handmaids and their children fore-
> most, and Leah and her children after, and Rachel
> and Joseph aftermost."

Rarely have God's people provided an act of such brazenness and callousness. If there was trouble the handmaids and their children would be fodder for the first blows with Leah and hers providing a secondary cushion. The prized family members, beloved wife Rachel and treasured young Joseph were afforded the presumed safety of the rear echelon. Doubtless all noticed this, and the crude fatherly ranking of sons wounded deeply the souls of the unfavored.

It was all for naught. Jacob bowed seven times before Esau, who then embraced Jacob and wept. All was forgiven. The brotherly bonds had been reestablished. Esau's growth had not been limited to money, flocks and herds, for he had assuredly grown as a man. After all the duplicity, the lying, the animosity, enmity and after all the years Jacob and Esau reconciled and parted as brothers.

Reconciliation and brotherly love were not to be the watchwords of Jacob's family, for as the family both grew and diminished the fixated emotion of hatred sank deeply into the souls of ten of Jacob's sons. Jacob himself began to age, and the elder ten sons reached full maturity with wives and children of their own. Whether by design, neglect or indifference events now proceed to provide a template with detailed examples and instructions on how to destroy your own family. We are reminded that the ten eldest sons were of Leah and two handmaids, while one, Joseph was the child of the beloved Rachel. Benjamin is likewise, but as a small boy is not yet a factor. Joseph was lavished and exalted incessantly by his adoring father. One of history's most famous garments, a beautiful coat of multiple colors was given Joseph by Jacob. This garment alone set him apart as someone special, yet it may have been subordinate to another factor in engendering brotherly animosity. As a seventeen-year-old Joseph would relate to his father the failures and missteps of his older brothers, all grown men. Effectively a boy was supervising ten men, and the reaction of the brothers, though severe, is explicable. Their hatred, extreme to the point that they "...could not speak peaceably unto him" was not assuaged by what happened next.

As was his father, Joseph was a dreamer – in a literal sense. Being seventeen and the dreams placing him in the glow of a radiant light he hastened to tell his brothers. The interpretation of the dreams was that someday these brothers would bow down to him as their superior. As would be expected no brotherly feelings were soothed by Joseph's proclamation and "...they hated him yet the more for his dreams and for his words." The brothers' hatred had now metastasized to the point where they determined to murder him with their cover story to Jacob being that a wild animal had killed him. Hearing of this the oldest, Reuben, was loathe to shed a brother 's blood and suggested that he be thrown into a dry water well to "teach him a lesson." With Joseph now at the bottom of an abysmal filthy pit by "happenstance" a caravan of Ishmaelites trekking to Egypt appeared. Upon Judah's instigation rather than experiencing fratricide Joseph was sold to the Ishmaelite traders for twenty pieces of silver.

For the ten brothers, Reuben, Judah and the others there loomed the lifelong consciousness of betraying a brother who was little more than a boy. To Jacob was assigned the role of a father thrown into a hell of agony and grief over the loss of his prized son. Awaiting Joseph was slavery.

Wise persons have a keen awareness of real talent and ability in others. Such a man was the captain of Pharaoh's personal guard, Potiphar, who purchased Joseph and brought him into his prosperous house. He soon realized the young man's extraordinary abilities and Divine favor and placed Joseph in the role of overseer of his house. All was placed in Joseph's control, including Potiphar's wife, who appreciated Joseph's other attributes. Not only was he a brilliant administrator, but also Joseph was handsome and well built, or "well favored" as the Bible so describes. Proving that the millennia may pass, and cultures alter but that human desires and emotions remain constant she seduced Joseph to "lie with me." He refused, reminding her that he was in the trust of both Potiphar and God and that this would be "...a great wickedness and sin against God." He fled from her presence but in doing so she grabbed his garment away from him. If the woman's lust could not be satisfied her wounded pride would and she cried "Rape!" Potiphar believed his wife and had Joseph banished to prison, but a special prison where Pharaoh's own prisoners were housed.

Prison is hardly the presumed launching point for success, but herein is found the exception which Joseph made. The young, talented and magnetic man won the attention and favor of the prison's warden and soon he was entrusted with its entire management. Two prisoners of note were soon consigned to the jail, the Pharaoh's own butler and baker, each of whom was troubled by inexplicable dreams. Joseph, the interpreter pf dreams and possessed of heaven's favor stepped forward and provided their meaning, i.e. the butler would soon be restored to his position and to Pharaoh's favor and the baker condemned and executed. As the butler left prison, Joseph bade him to remember him to Pharaoh, but the butler's silent ingratitude condemned Joseph to languish in prison for two more years. Finally, Pharaoh's troubles became Joseph's path of opportunity. The monarch had recurring nightmares and suddenly his butler's memory returned. He knew of a man in prison, a young man possessed of an uncanny talent for interpreting dreams, and so Joseph was beckoned to the throne of Pharaoh himself. Giving God the credit for his interpretive ability Joseph proceeded to foretell the next fourteen years of Egypt's history. Harvests would be good, and the land would provide plenty for seven years, but these good days would be abruptly terminated and followed by another seven years of drought, famine and starvation. Gather grain and other foods in the seven good years so that Egypt, greatest of all ancient lands, may survive during the seven lean years. Little imagination is required to know that Pharaoh was hearing an interpretation unwelcome to his ears, but this ruler was that rarity, whether ancient or modern, a ruler with wisdom. Keenly he listened to the recommendation God made through the voice of Joseph. Select one man to be over all the land, and for the seven good years stockpile the surplus production so that the land would not starve during the seven years famine. A wise Pharaoh knew that his man was standing in front of him, and thus Joseph was made ruler of Egypt. Pharaoh declared that "only in the throne will I be greater than thee..." and thus, a seventeen-year-old slave boy, an escapee from the murderous wrath of his brothers, had in the span of a few years effectively become the prime minister of the greatest power on earth.

Famine, though not totally eradicated even in the twenty-first century, haunted all ages past. The famine came, not just to Egypt, but also to the surrounding nations. Yet Egypt possessed grain and bread, and it became the source of life to many, a multitude which included the ten eldest sons of Jacob, whose land of Canaan was starving. Jacob dispatched the men (Benjamin, the now favorite son being left behind for his safety) to Egypt to buy the vital grain. So, the ten brothers, Joseph's would be murderers, kidnappers and slave dealers do as so many. They journey westward to Egypt expecting to procure grain and instead meet the governor, Joseph himself.

Joseph is now accorded a prize that few ever experience, and he witnesses a dream literally come true. The ten see the great Joseph and bow down before him. Now thirty years old, dressed and accoutered in the royal regalia of an Egyptian they know him not as their brother. Yet Joseph has the huge leverage of knowing them, verbally manhandles them and accuses them of being spies. The floods of emotions begin to rise within Joseph, and he demands of them as proof of their authenticity, the presence of their youngest brother Benjamin. In the meantime, Joseph holds brother Simeon as a surety for the fulfillment of a pledge to return with Benjamin. In private Joseph breaks down and weeps, an emotional catharsis fueled by his overhearing Reuben expressing his belief and guilt that they are being avenged for the presumed death of brother Joseph.

With Simeon bound and imprisoned the nine brothers return home to Jacob and relate the disaster that has befallen them. The aged patriarch is enraged and overwhelmed and initially and adamantly refuses to allow Benjamin to accompany them on any return to Egypt. Jacob bemoans his bereavement in losing Joseph, likely Simeon and then Benjamin. Reuben steps forward with a macabre offer. If we do not return with Benjamin, Reuben relates, take my own two sons and kill them, but Jacob still refuses. The narrative requires us to ponder and pose the question of how a family, whose patriarchs Abraham, Isaac and Jacob, all received God's special blessing, be reduced to where sons are bargaining with the lives of grandsons?

Regardless of Jacob's intransigence the famine continues, and the grain supply's exhaustion demands a response. Upon Judah's oath to offer his life and forever accept any blame, Jacob relents and all ten sons, including Benjamin, return to Egypt.

In a story structured by surprise upon surprise one of the greatest now occurs. Upon returning to Egypt Joseph has the ten brothers brought to his personal residence where a great luncheon feast awaits them. Shocked, bewildered and trembling with fear at first these sons of Jacob imagined that they had been brought here for some personal retribution. They continued to bow to Joseph, who assured them that they were safe and that their God had guided the situation. So, the meal began and immediately Joseph's eyes were fixed upon the one brother who had not betrayed him, now a young man, the beloved Benjamin. Not only were his eyes so affixed but also Joseph's heart as pent-up emotion overcame him, Joseph longed to embrace Benjamin but instead quickly ran to his private chamber, where the emotion took the path of tears. Joseph, though, had to play many parts, and the firm but fair young Egyptian ruler returned to the banquet, where all was laughter, merriment and camaraderie. Joseph likewise indulged himself with a bit of brotherly favoritism and directed that Benjamin be given a share of food five times greater than any of the other brothers.

Seemingly all is well, and the eleven brothers begin the return journey home to Canaan with their hearts lighter and their grain sacks heavier. As tumblers in a lock, though, another surprise clicks into place and Joseph's grip on his brothers tightens. Their grain sacks filled, and each topped with the money they had brought one sack contained an extra item. Joseph instructed his steward to place in Benjamin's sack his silver cup, which served as the pretext for halting the sojourn of Jacob's sons back to Canaan. The Egyptians overtake them and return them to face the wrath of the great ruler Joseph. They again bow and beg his belief that they would not be so foolish as to steal valuables from such a great man. Yet the fact was undeniable that the cup had been found in Benjamin's sack. Joseph dictated his "peace" terms. I will, he explained, retain Benjamin as my prisoner and the rest of you may return to your father.

Years ago, Joseph the beloved son of the treasured Rachel had effectively died to Jacob. Now, Jacob, the patriarch, the descendant of Abraham and Isaac was poised to lose the child of his old age, Benjamin. All, including Joseph, knew this would kill Jacob.

What had come of God's call of Abraham from Ur of the Chaldees? A great patriarchal line of Abraham, Isaac and Jacob had been established, but its heart was about to be torn away. The family, which had weathered so much, now stood on a precipice at the edge of a cliff. Would its destruction now be completed?

Chapter 3

THE REDEMPTION OF JUDAH

n infant either grows or dies. As beautiful and treasured is a baby the infant cannot so remain. He or she must grow physically, mentally and emotionally and must achieve some level of adult maturity without which either death or an incomplete life awaits. This is so plain that explanation and narrative is unnecessary. Without nourishment, care, and attention growth is stunted, and the infant perishes. It is difficult to imagine, harsh as it may sound, that in a utilitarian sense no creature in this world is more helpless or useless than a human infant. Still it is with the parents of children that this work is most concerned, but surprisingly the same principles applicable to the nurture and growth of babies likewise seem to be appropriate with the parents of those children. Both ancient and modern societies spoke and taught much on child raising and growth. Disappointingly, though, the sources of instruction for parental growth are far fewer. Modern bookshelves groan with the weight of guides, manuals and supposedly authoritative treatises on the manner in which parents should raise or "grow" their children, yet similar instruction on how the parent is to grow and mature are much scarcer. Fortunately, the one source that is not looking in such parental growth narratives is the most important, the Holy Bible.

One story which must be a piece placed in the long mosaic of the story of Abraham's descendants is that of a man of whom much is sounded but little studied. Judah was given a seemingly undistinguished place and echelon in the order of Jacob's sons, the story of which we now resume. He was the fourth son, borne of his mother Leah, the unfavored wife of Jacob, and ranking behind his older brothers Reuben, Levi and Simeon. As a child of Leah, Judah absorbed to the marrow of his bones what it meant to be an outsider in your own family, since it was Joseph and Benjamin who enjoyed the patriarchal favor. Our first glimpse of the character of this son of Jacob is chilling and stark.

Again, we are reminded of the story of the youthful Joseph being taken and bound by his ten older brothers, all of whom nursed a passionate hatred for the favored son, the "Golden Boy" of the family, who they now planned to murder. Save for the intervention of the oldest, Reuben, Joseph would have been slain on the spot. Biding their time, they cast him into a pit and then determined what should be done to him. Upon seeing the passing Midianite caravan it was the avaricious Judah who suggested that killing Joseph was shortsighted when he could just as easily be sold into slavery. So there the story of Joseph separated from that of his brothers for the next thirteen years, with the brothers' recompense being twenty pieces of silver. (How fitting that pieces of silver were received for an act of betrayal by a man named Judah). Still, an explanation for Joseph's absence had to be proffered to patriarch Jacob, as another killing occurred. The brothers slit the throat of a baby goat and smeared its blood on Joseph's prized coat of many colors. They took the coat to Jacob and explained that they had discovered it abandoned with Joseph doubtless "...rent in pieces" by a wild animal. All were then witness to their father Jacob's collapsing in agony and grief as he mourned the presumed death of the beloved Joseph. In an act of hypocrisy which ranks with any and all in the annals of history the other sons, including Judah, sought to "comfort" their inconsolable father. Though they were damaged by the unfortunate favoritism the callousness of watching a father dissolve in grief speaks ill of all the sons.

The young Judah has shown little in the way of character, and his moral future is beset by clouds of bleakness. The next Biblical encounter with Jacob describes a man who has grown into middle age and is himself a father and patriarch. Against God's warnings earlier he had married a Canaanite woman Shuah, by whom he fathered three sons, Er, Onan and Shelah. The impact of the first two sons on family history is uniformly bad. For an undisclosed transgression or character defect Er was slain by God himself. This left Onan as the oldest son in the family, and under the ancient tradition of levirate marriage he was obliged to marry Tamer, Er's widow. Instead, Onan crudely refused this obligation, which displeased God to the point of Onan's life being taken as well. Only Shelah of Judah's sons remained, but he was just a boy, far too young for marriage. Judah as patriarch of his dwindling family returned daughter-in-law Tamar to her father's house until Shelah came of marital age. Yet it did not happen. Even when Shelah reached adulthood he remained in the house of Judah, who had now become a widower with thoughts more pressing than the marriage of the wife of a long-deceased son.

Judah turned to the oversight of his flocks of sheep, but Tamar's mind and intentions turned otherwise as well. Removing the widow's garments of mourning she dressed herself otherwise and placed a veil upon her face, a cultural indication that she was available as a prostitute. She was aware of Judah's intended path to Timnath and so situated herself in an "open place." When Judah came by the widower he solicited her services, and the two struck a bargain. Tamar would receive a kid from Judah's flock after she fulfilled her portion of the bargain. Shrewdly though, she demanded a pledge for Judah's performance, and Judah provided Tamar a signet ring and tiny bracelets. He goes in and enjoys the still veiled Tamar's company and pleasures and fulfills the pledge by sending the kid from his flocks.

Judah, in strict adherence to their contracts sends a friend to retrieve the signet and bracelets, but his friend, Adullamite, cannot find her and returns to Judah empty handed. As low as Judah's character has sunk one more revelation will show the true depth of his depravity.

Three months pass, and Judah's servants inform him that his unmarried daughter-in-law Tamar is pregnant. The morally outraged and indignant Judah reacts with full patriarchal splendor and rage:

> "And Judah said, Bring her forth and let her be burnt."

Before being condemned Tamar reminds Judah that she is carrying a baby and she adds incidentally, here is your signet and bracelets. Judah is cornered, his grotesque deed revealed and morally he has been shamed. Perhaps, though, a corner has been turned in his deplorable conduct as a father and father-in-law as he speaks of himself and Tamar:

> "She hath been more righteous than I."

Usually a person's character is fully set and established at the stage of life that Judah has now reached. Changes of importance are rare, and often even minor modifications are not the norm. The scriptural record of Judah's life to this point is not favorable. Will a decline continue or is there a change on the horizon?

The true head of Jacob's family is, in fact, Jacob; however, the wise old patriarch is truly aged, and his days grow shorter in number. Who will succeed him in this vital position as patriarch? Jacob knows that only eleven sons remain, for Joseph has long since perished. Of the remaining eleven, the now favored Benjamin is still little more than a boy. We are now reminded of the imperiled family as it stands helpless and prostrates itself before the mighty ruler of Egypt. The men tremble with fear and bewilderment, bowing before a mighty power who has the say of life and death over all of them. Their own father Jacob, frail and aged, is absent and can no longer protect them.

Further, some or maybe even all have surmised that this God of our Fathers, Abraham, Isaac and Jacob has been deathly silent and has stood silent while they are innocently and falsely accused. Yet, great opportunities present themselves in such moments of mortal peril, and true character and leadership was now writ large before them all.

As our gaze returns to Joseph's house we see these eleven brothers bereft of hope and any means of clearing themselves from a false charge of theft. The great man of Egypt, though, is not a man who seeks to drain from a situation every drop of vengeance and retribution. Alternatively, he explains what will transpire. Ten of the brothers may return to their native land and to peace, but the one "thieving" brother shall remain in Egypt as Joseph's personal slave. These ten men, the sons of Leah, Bilhah and Zilpah, may return to Canaan, but to the patriarch Jacob the cherished sons of Rachel, both Joseph and Benjamin shall be no more. The ugly, poisoned fruit of family favoritism, begun decades and generations earlier, has now fully ripened. One son of Jacob, Joseph, holds in his hands the power to fully destroy Jacob's family and with that destruction Jacob himself. This is not mere supposition but is a certainty that will occur unless there comes forward some force or someone to redeem the fortunes of a family mined in tragedy. The true leader and patriarch of the family is both aged and absent. In a culture in which age and rank were given great sway, we look to the eldest sons for action and see none. These three, Reuben, Levi and Simeon, are all silent. Does such a redeemer even exist?

The fourth son of Jacob cautiously approaches the ruler, petitions for an abatement of his anger and requests leave to speak. Judah effectively has now become the parent, the surrogate father speaking for all the brothers. Whatever their sins (and they are as scarlet) these ten men have been callously and dreadfully wronged by their father. The searing white heat of the spotlight of the moment, of history and even of eternity now bears down upon Judah.

He carefully and thoroughly relates both the story of his family and its sojourn into Egypt, its bearing the false accusations of being spies and the attendant loneliness of their father Jacob, who waits at home, alone with the bitterness of having lost Joseph and the fear of the same with the "child" of his old age, "Benjamin". The guilt, pain and hurt that drove Judah to utter these words must have been of gargantuan proportions. The guilt from instigating the sale into slavery of Joseph and then the deception of Joseph's death to Jacob and the paid and hurt of knowing that he, Judah, as well as the others, were of secondary value to their father.

In revealing the inner workings and history of his family to a supposed stranger Judah attains an astonishing candor. He plainly tells the great man of a simple fact. If we return to Canaan without our brother Benjamin, our father Jacob will die. The silence, atmosphere and tension in the room must have grown oppressive as Judah speaks:

> "Now, therefore, I pray thee, let they servant abide
> instead of the lad a bondman to my lord;
> and let the lad go with his brethren.
> For how shall I go up to my father, and the lad be
> not with me? Less peradventure
> I see the evil that shall come on my father."

By this expression Judah has injected into this family a quality conspicuously rare, and that is the spirit of sacrifice. By the sacrifice of my life, Judah pledges, the others will be redeemed and saved. Well had Judah learned the meaning of the phrase spoken once by a very wise person. "To be a good parent the first word that must be learned is sacrifice."

Judah's discourse now gives way to a scene that is in the front rank of drama in the entirety of the Old Testament. In actuality, the tension and drama, which has built for countless years, is almost more than the narrative may bear. Almost, but not quite. Joseph's emotions break, and he cries for all save his brothers to leave the room. Alone now with his own blood he reveals his identity and begins to weep. Stunned as if they had literally seen one come back from the grave the brothers are drawn near to each other and Joseph explains:

"I am Joseph, your brother, whom ye sold into
Egypt."

He dwells not on his degradation, humiliation and suffering and his grasp that though his brothers had meant his maltreatment for evil God was the true author of his presumed misfortune, trip to Egypt and rise to power. Not for the last time does God employ a deliverer, for as Joseph explains:

"God sent me before you to preserve you a posterity in the earth, and to save your lives by a great deliverance."

The emotional catharsis of this family is not yet exhausted for Joseph embraces and kisses his beloved younger brother Benjamin and kisses each of his brothers. He commissions his family to return to Canaan, inform father Jacob of these marvelous events and bring Jacob and all the family to Egypt where they shall dwell as honored residents.

In a tribute to Joseph's character not only is the sovereign Pharaoh pleased with these happenings, but likewise (and tellingly) so were the servants. When told the amazing tale of these events the aged Jacob's stirs with excitement, and all "...see the spirit of Jacob their father revive." A great migration to Egypt transpires and essentially the young new nation of Israel is transplanted from Canaan to Goshen. The reunion of father and son of Jacob and Joseph, is marked by unrestrained tears, and its emotional depth is better imagined than described.

Upon the later death of Jacob fear enveloped the brothers of Joseph as they reckoned that with the protection of their father Jacob removed Joseph would turn upon them again. Not so, assured

Joseph, kindly explaining that if this was all God's plan he was happy with the cycle of events. So, the entire family of Jacob of Isaac and of Abraham now settled into Egypt and there remained for four hundred years, when God's plans enfold at a larger perspective.

From the time of Judah's great soliloquy before Joseph and the other brothers the scriptures make no specific reference to Judah's actions and activities. Now, at the conclusion of Abraham's departure from Ur of the Chaldees to the settlement of his grandchildren and great grandchildren in Egypt provides the opportunity for a brief review of Judah's life.

First impressions often set the tone of our views on a person, and the color of the early views of Judah is gray, perhaps even fading into black. His idea not to murder Joseph, but instead sell him to Midianite traders for twenty pieces of silver seems to have its genesis not in mercy, but in avarice. Further he was a full participant in the lie foisted upon his father Jacob, a lie that plunged Jacob into agony and despair over the presumed loss of Joseph.

We are provided no direct views of Judah in the role of a father, and to make judgments from the little we know is hazardous – hazardous, yet permitted. Judah's first two sons, Er and Onan, were literally struck dead by God; however, perhaps contrary to mistaken beliefs the God of the Old Testament only infrequently took lives. It would be totally improper and unfair to attribute the wickedness of these two sons directly to their father Judah, his teachings and character, yet it would be impossible to not conjecture. Did a poor father produce evil sons? He was apparently remiss in failing to make his third son Shelah available in a timely manner for a levirate marriage to his daughter-in-law. It is in his dealings with her, Tamer, that the character of Judah is viewed at its nadir.

For any man in any culture at any time to seek the services of a prostitute is as degrading to him as is the prostitute's profession to her. Yet Judah's lust demanded satisfaction, and so he received it, but in the dark abyss of his behavior lay the seeds for moral rebirth. The hypocrisy of condemning Tamar for prostitution was repulsive, but Judah's surprise in finding that he was her partner seemed to open his eyes. My sin is the greater, he acknowledged, a wise and rare admission for anyone.

Maybe we are overly hasty when we aver that no examples exist of Judah in the role of parent, for on his final stage in Genesis we effectively witness him in this role. Eleven men, substantial men, husbands and fathers, stood and also were prostrate before the great ruler of Egypt, and they were totally helpless in the face of his seemingly whimsical conduct. How could they possibly return home, their hands now having forfeited into slavery Benjamin, the last of the sons of the beloved Rachel? The true leader and patriarch of the family, Jacob, remained at home, effectively poised to die upon hearing the impending news of disaster in Egypt. Another was needed to step forward in the place of Jacob and reconcile the brothers with the Egyptian ruler and pacify his anger. It was not to be either Reuben, Levi or Simeon, the three oldest brothers. Judah stepped forward, accepted blame and offered the sacrifice of himself for the freedom and redemption of the remainder of his brothers.

It was not Reuben, Levi or Simeon who succeeded Jacob in this great line of patriarchs, Abraham, Isaac and Jacob, for in fact, the successor came to be Judah. But what of Judah as a father? The disgraceful union of Judah and Tamar is now recalled, and it is remembered that Tamar had become pregnant by Judah. Tamar, though, was not just pregnant, but she gave birth to twin sons, Perez and Zerah. This fourth son of Jacob makes one more appearance, for on his deathbed Jacob so blessed Judah: "Judah, your brothers shall praise you... and thy father's sons shall bow down before you."

The Tribe of Judah would become the dominant tribe of twelve in the nation of Israel and the name Judah itself lives in the names of their descendants, the Jews. Judah's direct lineage would include the shepherd David, who rose to become Israel's greatest king and fourteen generations thereafter, the true Redeemer, Jesus Christ.

Chapter 4

ELI AND SAMUEL: FAULTY AND FAULTED FATHERS

*T*his is the story of two fathers and the travails of fatherhood. One of the men was a mentor to the other, this mentor being a good, decent man, and his protégé became one of the noteworthy figures of the Old Testament and Israel's greatest judge. An enormous amount of the lives of each man was given to the labors and pains of fatherhood, but few moments of triumph in this sphere of life are recorded. Yet, the story commences not with fathers and sons nor any man but in the desperate desire of a childless woman for a son.

In the 1000's BC a polygamous man lived in the hill country of Ephraim, one of the smaller of Israel's tribes. His name was Elkanah, and although in these ancient times God permitted polygamy it fell short of the ideal standard of marriage. The spousal dynamic among Elkanah and his two wives, Peninah and Hannah is another proof of this. Although Elkanah treated both well his greater love was apparently given to Hannah; however, this love and geniality was not shared between the two wives. Peninah had considered herself blessed by bearing children for Elkanah, but she mocked the childless Hannah "...because the Lord had shut up her womb." In a culture in which childbearing was considered the most significant worth of a woman the disconsolate Hannah was comforted by husband Elkanah. In a phrase which likely bears more clumsiness than egotism Elkanah asked Hannah to consider that "...am not I better than ten sons?" Bereft of child, on the last day of the family's annual pilgrimage to the temple at Shiloh, Hannah, embittered in soul and spirit made a vow in a strange tear-laden prayer to God that if He gave her a son she would return the favor by dedicating that son to God. Hannah's petition was granted, she gave birth to a boy named Samuel, and her love for both her son and God set the moral tone and history of Israel for two generations. Upon the infant's being weaned Hannah fulfilled her covenant and brought Samuel to live and be influenced and raised by the priest Eli.

Eli, in common with much of humanity, was a man with a decidedly mixed record. He possessed the knowledge, character and priestly position to be entrusted with the care and growth of a surrogate son who, in point of fact, would mature into one of the giant figures in the story of Israel. His charge, Samuel, would assume the role of judge of the nation for forty years and prove to be a man above reproach, universally revered by his countrymen and the man God selected to anoint the first two Kings of Israel. Obviously, Eli assumed with seriousness his assigned duties with Samuel, and his fatherly influence undoubtedly was for the good. Eli was entrusted not only with the raising of Samuel but also with the vital position of priest, a role he held and in which he performed well and effectively for forty years. In no way was Eli a neophyte when it came to responsibility and that experience extended to fatherhood itself. With Samuel Eli was not a parent in training, for he already was the father of two sons, Hophni and Phineas, each of whom was also a priest and presumably were following in the footsteps of their father. How false and unknowing would such a presumption prove. In the sometimes stark but yet strangely and beautifully descriptive language of the Old Testament these two young priests were "sons of Belial," or literally, "worthless men." Yet they were not worthless because of their parental lineage, not worthless because of their priests' responsibilities but rather worthless due to their grotesque character.

As part of the narrative of the story thanks must be offered to Hophni and Phineas for making their conduct still so easy to visualize even three thousand years later. Woven into the fabric of the Law of Moses was the obligation of sacrifice, a requirement that was fulfilled in part by journeys to the temple to offer animal sacrifice. Customarily when a Jew offered this sacrifice the meat of the animal was roasted and the priests received as their payment a portion of the sacrifice. Not so with Hophni and Phineas, as before the sacrifice was offered the two priests demanded the entirety of what was to be sacrificed for these two contemptible priests "...abhorred the offering of the Lord." Then showing an expertise that perhaps reached its zenith in the modern Mafia should any man refuse to give them what they demanded it would be taken "... by force." They justly earned acknowledgment as history's first and still among its greatest "shakedown artists." One act alone, though, no matter how nefarious, corrupt or disgusting rarely makes a worthless man. Another vice which the sons of Eli possessed and unfortunately shared with too many of history's clerical orders was sexual vice. The would literally:

> "...lay with the women that assembled at the door of
> the tabernacle of the congregation."

In all these abominations Eli was no participant. Yet, God was displeased with him, the displeasure being so intense that He announced that He would make an end of Eli's house. God's pronouncements here are so thorough, so encompassing and yet simultaneously so succinct that they require quotation in full:

> "For I have told him that I will judge his house for
> ever for the iniquity which he knoweth;

because his sons made themselves vile, and he
restrained them not."

Historically and theologically the focus of both scholarship and lessons of warning has been the phrase "...he restrained them not," and it is upon these few words we will place our focus. Eli's performance as a father of Hophni and Phineas as children and youths is substantially a matter of conjecture and speculation, substantially but not entirely. The two were not lacking in religious training and in the influence of the Mosaical Law for essentially, they were, to employ a later phrase, raised in the church building itself. Religious devotion, piety the importance of the maintenance of high moral values likely were not strangers to them. Further, the scriptures make no revelation that Eli himself was lax in his priestly duties or was particularly immoral himself. After all, he was entrusted to care for Samuel. The apparent missing piece in the tools of fatherhood which Eli possessed was his failure to restrain his sons, or more precisely his failure to discipline. Herein has the controversy always been located. What is proper and appropriate discipline? Always this has been a subject of great human concern and its theories of emphasis and propriety are legion, far more numerous than a single written volume could summarize. At the risk of gross oversimplification, though, we posit that traditionally two streams of thought have run parallel to each other.

The first theory is what might be denominated the "Old School" approach of sparing the rod and spoiling the child. Often this is accompanied by a detailed list of rules and regulations, the strict adherence to which is required and harshly punished if breached. The more extreme proponents of this seemingly envision a family unit which is regimental in form and militaristic in parent-child relationships. The principles of the second theory of fatherhood and child raising are perhaps colored with more moderate tones, emphasizing self-esteem, freedom of expression and the cultivation of individuality (or at least the individuality which the parent desires). These ideas have often been coupled, sometimes unfairly, with permissiveness. On and on continues the timeless and endless debate regarding fatherhood, but as it is applicable to Eli's parenting skills it misses an essential factor. Except for the setting of the father-son relationship the Bible provides not one fact, not a scintilla of evidence of Eli as a parent of his children when they were, in fact, children. The scriptures offer us the bold, stark, unvarnished statement that Eli failed to restrain his sons. Yet in the context in which this truth is delivered it appears that this information is applicable to Eli's role as high priest when his young sons were adult priests themselves, not as the father of two infants or toddlers.

What is more easily inferred from the vile character of Hophni and Phineas is that Eli may have been guilty of fatherly malfeasance by failing to inculcate into his sons the most effective, and in most ways the only lasting form of restraint or discipline, that is self-discipline. In those matters of priestly and Biblical concern the two erring sons had none of this essential quality.

Consistently and historically it has often been assumed that Eli was an "easy" father, permissive and lacking in the will and/or ability to discipline his children, yet the scriptures do not necessarily provide support and authority for this view. From the safe plane of observation given to us from the remove of three thousand years it is easy to condemn Eli. Just as easy it is for us to harshly berate by words or attitudes our contemporaries when we perceive their apparent failures as parents. The best of sons and daughters may have been given copious religious instruction (as were Eli's sons), consistent and prolonged exposure to persons who serve God (as were Eli's sons) and even attain responsible positions in the church, or the temple, as Eli's sons. What makes them abhorrent is none of these factors, but rather their own attitudes and characters. Not only life but the Bible itself is replete with men and women, with one or more serious parents, who themselves stumbled and fell morally. In almost all, if not the entirety of instances, fathers and mothers must shoulder a portion of the blame, but to automatically assign the role of parental criminal to them is faulty and often plainly wrong. Likely Eli failed often as a father, but even more probable is the reality that Hophni and Phineas owned natural character and innate proclivities that led them to become hedonistic thugs wearing priestly robes.

The finale to the story of Hophni and Phineas is certainly fitting. As was common at this time the Israelites were locked in a war with their dread enemy, the Philistines. Israel early had lost 4,000 men and the people and their elders called for a special intervention. The most treasured and valued property in all Israel was the ark of the covenant, and it was summoned from the temple in Shiloh. Its procession to the field of battle at Ebenezer was led by Hophni and Phineas. The Israelite people were delirious with joy, but the emotions of God, as is so often the case, did not synchronize themselves with His people. The ark was sacred, a part of the worship ceremony, and it contained the Ten Commandments, yet it was being employed as a sort of talisman for victory. Israel was overwhelmed in battle, 30,000 men perished, and the sons of Eli likewise met their fate. Upon hearing of the demise of his two sons, however corrupt they were, the aged Eli, now blind, was overcome, fell, broke his neck and thus perished. The priestly line of Eli, Hophni and Phineas was no more.

Although Israel had seen the last of Eli, Hophni and Phineas it had not felt the end of Eli's influence for his pupil, Samuel, had assumed the role of judge, and as facts would have it the final judge of Israel before it was transformed into a monarchy. From the cradle Samuel was surrounded by good influences, commencing with a sacrificial mother in Hannah, a mentor, priest and surrogate father in Eli and an immersion in Mosaical laws and traditions such that he became not only the judge but a great leader and the nation's first great prophet. To offer more than a brief biographical sketch of Samuel's accomplishments requires not a separate essay or chapter, but a separate volume.

What followed Samuel's unique childhood is a litany of accomplishment. As referenced he assumed the role of Israel's final judge in a period of the nation's being in mortal combat with its traditional foe, the dread Philistines. As the Philistine wars worsened and took more and more out of Israel he and God had to succumb to a popular demand that the ancient ordained government of Israel give way to a monarchy, "just as all the other nations had." He had to endure what to many men would be an indignity, of having to anoint his successor, Saul, as king because the people had decided that Samuel had "failed." Samuel and Saul actually develop a personal relationship somewhat akin to father and son, and Saul's own failure as a man and as a king must have placed a deep emotional scar upon Samuel. Yet it was this man, the great judge and prophet, to whom God entrusted the work of anointing the second king and the successor to Saul. That Samuel did and in the winds of skepticism from the new anointee's family Samuel marked David as Israel's next king. Further, to add to his accomplishments he was the author of two of the Bible's most studied and interesting books, I and II Samuel. Quite a life, and the activity which took the bulk of his time has barely been mentioned.

Samuel lived in the small town of Ramah, but this was seemingly as much a base of operations as it was a real home. Annually he went on preaching and judging tours throughout all of Israel, and these undoubtedly assumed not only his time but much of his mental energy and dedication.

No man or woman, then or now, is flawless, but Samuel's conduct in a host of duties is uniformly impeccable. Further, if such a title were given this great man would be in the first tier of those nominated for the title, "Busiest Man in the Bible." All these factors made up Samuel, but they were not all of Samuel. Like most men of all generations and cultures, Samuel was a family man and as the bard spoke, "...there's the rub." All humanity is allocated twenty-four hours to a day and seven days a week, and as great and important as was Samuel he was given no exception. Undoubtedly with his job or "career" as we might more commonly reference today Samuel was away from his home in Ramah a substantial portion of the time. Rare would be a modern man, including fathers, who could not instantly grasp Samuel's dilemma, often expressed in some variation of "I must make a living and provide for my family, but also I need to spend time with my family."

Since the subject of Samuel's family has been introduced let us subject it to a review and examination. By his wife (unfortunately anonymous in the scriptures) Samuel had two sons, Joel and Abijah, both of whom proved to be worthy successors. Not worthy successors to Samuel or Eli for that matter but worthy successors to the contemptible sons of Eli, Hophni and Phineas. Nothing is known of their childhood or the parental techniques employed by Samuel and their mother. The aged Samuel, tired and understandably wearying of his long career and duties as a judge appointed his sons as judges over Israel. Their judicial record is capsulized in one starkly comprehensible sentence:

> "And his sons walked not in his ways, but turned
> aside after lucre (money), and took bribes
> and perverted judgment."

The above is a summary of judicial conduct that may easily be tacked upon the most corrupt judges in history, many be their number. From a comfortable perch of sight some three millennia hence the quick judgment of Samuel has invariably been that although he was among Israel's greatest he must have been severely flawed as a father. Out natural bent is to assign blame and dangerously is this manifested in those circumstances, such as here, where we are granted only partial knowledge. Theoretically Samuel could have been history's worst father to his young sons as they were growing and maturing. This is unlikely to be true, though, and as with Eli, any blame to Samuel attaches later in life after all concerned parties were grown men. Coincidentally where the strongest case for fault in Samuel occurs in the same stage of life as it did with Eli.

Undoubtedly the two sons of Samuel were not mere boys or callow youths when Samuel appointed them judges. Whatever his merits and standing as a father – Samuel should have been more aware of the low and base character of his sons, a character that had to be open and observed even before their judgeships. His error cost Israel grievously, and surely many individuals paid unfair prices for having been judged by Joel and Abijah.

An essential question, still relevant and extant, is whether the conduct of Eli and Samuel as fathers paved the pathway for the development of four defective men such as Hophni, Phineas, Joel and Abijah. Strictly as fathers neither man may be condemned, simply because the facts which would relevantly bear on the query are omitted. Each father, but especially Samuel, was faced with the dilemma shared by all fathers and which has only been exacerbated by modernity. In the tersest of terms, it is rendered "How can I do my job and still have time to be a good father." Although many counselors, mentors, clergy and pundits daily strain to supply answers to this question it is doubtful that an answer, at least a simple one, will ever be found.

Almost all fathers and conscientious workers will be forced to admit that the activity which during a lifetime consumed the most hours is, by an overwhelming margin, work. Since most now dwell in advanced economics urbanized societies work means absence from sons and daughters. No longer is it common for fathers and sons to work side-by-side in the fields or for a son to apprentice his father's trade or profession. For most those times have receded into memory. A father's work often equals a father's absence but not necessarily the absence of a father's influence. Samuel was gone from his home in Ramah a substantial portion of time, but surely his influence remained. Most certainly did his sons know his character, of his integrity as a judge and of his full commitment to God. Maybe Samuel was remiss in devoting too little time to his sons in favor of a full devotion to his profession, and if he did great or not he must not escape censor. Maybe he was not. Samuel faced the same reality that all fathers and all mothers must confront with their children. The parent deals with, teaches and loves his own offspring, but they are sentient beings, independent and each possesses his or her own mind.

Any failings of Samuel as a father, whether real or perceived, are dwarfed by the overall character of the great man. Surely for Samuel is vouchsafed a place if heaven, where he will enjoy and revel in a Father who will lavish him with an eternity of time.

Chapter 5

SAUL, THE UNDESERVING PARENT

A long time past a certain phrase worked itself into the English language that remains in common (though, as with many phrases, inappropriate) usage yet today. Primarily its employment is utilized to describe a person, a situation, an event or a result that is so sad and dispiriting that it be called a "Greek tragedy." The ancient Greek authors of tragedy, men such as Sophocles and Aeschylus, Athenians who penned many dramas which are still performed and studied, tragic plays which provide a wealth of wisdom and a lexicon of terms still extant. These men, though, lived and wrote in the 400's BC, some five to six centuries after a real human tragedy that for drama and pathos surpassed anything written by these men, great as they were. It was not a Greek, but rather a human tragedy. In reality, however, in the spectrum of history nationality plays only a minor role, for it is the tragedy of one man's rise and prominence which collapses into moral disintegration. Accompanying this collapse is his deterioration and failures, even malignity, as a father. Initially, though, we must see how this man rose to a pinnacle of fame and power.

After fourteen judges and many generations of a divinely ordained theocracy the people of Israel were growing restless. The last of the judges had placed into judicial positions his two scheming, corrupt and extortionate sons, Joel and Abijah, and their conduct helped the Israelites to quickly forget the greatness of their father, Samuel. To add to the unrest, as noted in Chapter Four, Israel had suffered a crushing defeat by the Philistines at Ebenezer. The elders of Israel now demanded of Samuel to "...make us a king to judge us like all the nations." A crestfallen Samuel was assured by God that it was not Samuel but God Himself who suffered the people's rejection. A king they would have, though, as God acceded to the popular demand. Prior to the monarch's selection the Israelites had to absorb a prophetic warning as to the nature of their king. In history's first recorded diatribe on the hazards of Big Government, Samuel warned that their king would conscript your sons into his armies, he would nationalize the best of your lands, he would increase your taxes and the oppression would be so great that you will cry for relief from God. Nonetheless, the people had cast the die, and God told Samuel "...make them a king," so Samuel went forth to find Israel's first monarch.

If ever a man seemed to be fashioned to be a king, it was Saul. He is described simply as the most handsome young man in Israel, taller than his contemporaries and with a commanding presence yet an attractively and engagingly modest manner. When tabbed to be king by Samuel he modestly deferred but nonetheless was eventually anointed first king of Israel.

The young King Saul commenced his tenure and reign as a warrior king in a brilliant blaze. Israel was in a crisis with the presence of a strong Philistine army ever looming. The Philistines in the west were an ever-present peril, but first Saul had a military crisis on another front. Saul had temporarily returned to farming even after being chosen king, and soon the Ammonites besieged a city called Jabesh-gilead, east of the Jordan River. The town was ready to capitulate, especially after the King of the Ammonites threatened to gouge out the right eye of every inhabitant. Saul, bringing in oxen from his fields heard this, was inflamed with anger and zeal and sent out a call for militia from all Israel. The plea received a positive answer, the Ammonites were repelled, and Saul had his first moment in the sun as a hero.

Soon, one of his generals, a man named Jonathan, who was also Saul's son, captured a Philistine stronghold in Gaba, an action which sparked a Philistine response that nearly overwhelmed the Israelites. The ancient City of Gilgal was chosen by Saul as a rallying point for his amateur army, but his troops began abandoning him as desertion skyrocketed. Saul, a political figure only as king, in fear of military disaster, then usurped the Biblical role of the priesthood by offering burnt sacrifices to God. God was so incensed that through Samuel he informed Saul that "...your kingdom shall not continue."

As if to solidify God's opinion of Saul, the king commits a more egregious sin. Exemplary of Old Testament Divine fury God had ordered Saul to turn his attention to the Amalekites, historic pagan enemies of Israel, and not only defeat them but put every Amalekite man, woman, child and domestic animal to the sword. Saul defeated the Amalekite army, but in an early display of the self-will that would lead to his destruction spared the Amalekite king and the animals, which the king told Samuel he intended to sacrifice to God. An exasperated Samuel then uttered those immortal words:

"To obey is better than sacrifice"

The future removal of Saul's kingship was reconfirmed, but eventually Saul, still King, had to turn his and his army's attention to its prime enemy, the Philistines. The two armies gathered for a pitched battle at a place called Shochoh, and the valley of Elah lay between the two hosts. It is with hesitancy that we denominate a place, a time or an event as a turning point, but common as is the terminology it is sometimes appropriate. Both the army of Israel and Israel's king were intimidated by the Philistine hordes and a special soldier, Goliath of Gath, a giant who for forty days running hurled defiance and words of mockery towards the Israelite soldiers and their God. None of the Israelites answered Goliath's challenge for one-on-one combat as they all cowered before a man said to be over nine feet tall.

Fortunately for Israel but unfortunately for King Saul the moment now provides the entrance of perhaps the singularly most arresting figure in the entire Old Testament, David, the youth who will slay Goliath and succeed Saul as king. Unlike the remainder of Saul's soldiers and Saul himself, when David heard Goliath's taunts and cursing of God he queried:

> "Who is this uncircumcised Philistine, that he
> should defy the armies of the living God?"

One of the Bible's and history's most famous legendary stories now finds the young David as the slayer of Goliath and the new hero of Israel. It is not this essay's purpose to relate the full history of David nor of Saul. For our narrative purposes suffice it to say that the praise Saul had known as a young king had now been commandeered by David, a rising military star in Saul's army, and it was David who could revel in the acclaim"

> "And the women answered one another as they
> played, and said, Saul hath slain his thousands, and
> David his ten thousands."

Neither the pages of the Bible nor Israel's history had yet revealed one who had the charisma of David. He was Godly, an accomplished warrior as a young man, a musician, the author of much of the Book of Psalms and strikingly handsome with a physical beauty celebrated by artists yet today. Women literally fell at his feet, and men recognized his natural leadership talents. King Saul, though, saw his own successor and developed a jealousy so heated that it burned through Saul's own soul and eventually destroyed him. No less did it begin to corrupt Saul's character as a father.

A man's downfall and demise may be harsh and sudden. He may be strong and high principled one moment, and on the turning of one terrible decision destroy himself. Not so with Saul, for his deterioration and moral erosion played itself out in quite public and conspicuous ways over the next two decades. The reasons for Saul's long slow physical, mental and spiritual death spiral are long debated, yet they may be categorized under three themes. Initially Saul was now working independently of God, for the Divine Spirit had forsaken the King. Saul's full capacity as a man and a monarch could never be attained, and he would live the remainder of his days in the shadow of his brilliant and anointed successor, David. Saul was a broken man, but he retained a great intelligence and perception of his surroundings. David, not Saul, was the anointed of God and the darling of the people, and thus begat the jealousy which would essentially drive insane the once promising young king. Handicapped though he was and as events would plainly proclaim growing increasingly imbalanced mentally Saul still retained a formidable arsenal of weapons with which to advance his cause.

Arranged marriages, especially among the royal and noble classes, are nothing new in history, and in a sense remain extant even today. Saul sought the advantages offered by monarchial power and reached for a foothold into the house of David. In his older daughter Merab he was certain he had found one and offered her in marriage to the young glamorous David. David, though, declined the offer for he had his eyes and heart set on another girl, Michal, Saul's younger daughter. Saul exacted a price for giving the hand of Michal to David. Bring me physical evidence that you have killed one hundred Philistines. Saul told David without question felt that the marital betrothal to Michal was itself being conditioned upon certain death for David. Saul's foe, though, was no ordinary prospective son-in-law and after accepting the King's offer David returns with evidence of having slain two hundred Philistines. Saul's bluff was called, and Michal became the bride of David. Although kingly politics contributed to this marriage, it was a love match, for each was truly pledged to each other-in the beginning. Saul, though, saw Michal as not so much a daughter but a potential spy in David's bed. Not only did Michal refuse this role but she sided David to escape from one of her father's endless murderous rages. David, who proved to be one of history's great escape artists, now lived in a lengthy period of exile, away from Saul and his murdering desires and away from Michal.

Now that the first rush of youthful ardor and passion that Michal and David shared began to fade, David took himself many women, several of whom he made his wives. Saul meanwhile continued his reign as king and his concurrent contemptible run as a father. Effectively and unilaterally annulling Michal's marriage he gave her again in marital bonds to a man named Palti, a man who loved her but for whom her love remained unrequited. Michal's woes continue unabated. Following Saul's death David determines that though he has now collected many wives he cherishes the return of his first love, Michal. In a scene both heart wrenching and anger inducing Michal is forcibly taken from a weeping Palti and returned to David, who is now King. But to what purpose?

Among David's initial acts as king was to return the ark of the covenant, the most sacred symbol of the Israelite's religion to the tabernacle in Jerusalem. The day of return came and David, dressed in priestly garments, danced before the ark as it came to rest in its rightful place. Michal, watching all this, accosted David for his "unkingly" behavior before everybody from God to the young servant girls:

> "How glorious was the King of Israel today, who
> uncovered himself today in the handmaids of his
> servants..."

David not to be outdone in a venomous exchange now assured Michal of two facts, that she would remain childless and then crudely that David would have no difficulty finding comfort with the young girls.

Michal was born with as bright a future as any in the Bible, but her father Saul offered her as a pawn to his rival David. In an age when women were publicly reticent about their feelings she expressed hers and at the risk of life and limb remained loyal to her husband. Effectively sold again in marriage to Palti she was forcibly removed and as a chattel returned to David. It all began with her father, Saul. Blessed with two daughters Merab and Michal, he saw them as pieces in a board game with David. As a father to daughters Saul never demonstrated love but rather his own sordid desire for self-aggrandizement.

The repugnance of Saul's conduct toward his daughter Michal was, unfortunately, no aberration. In a different arena, but with ultimately the same objectives its venality was matched, if not actually surpassed by his father-son relationship with son Jonathan. As much as any man or woman in history it was consigned to Jonathan the role of the classic man "caught in the middle" between two persons, each of whom he loved. Although it seemingly was of small consequence to Saul, Jonathan was ever loyal to his father. The son never betrayed the father though his opportunities to do so were great and often easily grasped. History, even Bible history, naturally prods its students to consider the "might have been" and "never was". Jonathan, a royal prince after his father was chosen king, never was king himself although he might have been. If his kingship had reflected his character he would have been one of Israel's greatest, for as a man he has few equals in the Old Testament.

Jonathan was already a responsible military leader in Saul's army when David made his entrance in the clash with Goliath. Doubtless he was somewhat older than David and the immediate hatred and jealousy which his father Saul felt for the young hero easily could have been absorbed and amplified by Jonathan.

After all he was the royal prince, and by ancient custom and practice could not Jonathan easily have reasoned that he, not David, should be the next King of Israel? Instead is as beautiful and lasting a description of friendship as the world has seen we are told:

"(T)he soul of Jonathan was knit with the soul of David, and Jonathan loved him as his own soul."

Beautiful words they are, but even the most elegant and moving language is meaningless if contradicted or unsupported by action. Jonathan, the son of a man who nurtured an unrestrained murderous hatred in his heart, did no dishonor to such flowing words. Instead, Jonathan, who knew that he would never himself be king:

> "...stripped himself of the robe that was upon him,
> and gave it to David, and his garments even to his
> sword, and to his bow, and to his sash."

The appearance, anointing and rise of young David was already an insurmountable roadblock to any hopes Jonathan may have entertained of being the sovereign, but his character did not become embittered. He accepted his roles, difficult parts, and performed each with exemplary grace and magnificence. Obviously accepting God's will for his young friend David to be anointed the next king, Jonathan never wavered in his friendship and commitment to David. Friendship itself, for all its pleasures and rewards, can often prove burdensome. Yet the greatest of Jonathan's burdens came not from his young friend David, but rather from his own father.

Thrice Jonathan was almost victim of the rage of the murderous Saul. In an early clash with the Philistines Saul had decreed that no soldier in the army would eat before the Philistines had suffered total defeat. Jonathan, showing military leadership of a high order led a small group of soldiers that defeated a Philistine outpost, provoking a panic throughout the remainder of the Philistine army. The famished Jonathan, unaware of the fasting edict of his father, ate some honey and strictly speaking broke the King's decree. Military victory or not, son or not, King Saul, perhaps also growing jealous of his own son wanted Jonathan executed. Jonathan, though, was now a popular hero with his day in the sun, and the people and cooler heads dissuaded Saul from his intended act of murder and idiocy. Jonathan in Saul's heart and mind had now joined the ever-burgeoning ranks of the King's enemies. Yet it is Saul's mind alone that Jonathan's disloyalty lurks like a demon, but in Jonathan's conscience and heart he remains loyal to the anointed kingship of his father.

Saul's anger and hatred continues to flare against any and all, and especially Jonathan, who one day must dodge a sword thrown at him by his father. Surely most sons would have broken entirely with a father who had attempted twice to murder them, but Jonathan was not most sons. The incentive to leave the royal house of King Saul was highly intense, and that incentive was heightened by the status of Jonathan's friend David for many years. His own life imperiled by the king's insane jealousy David became a fugitive from Saul, living everywhere and anywhere to escape certain death from Saul. Yet David was not a lone fugitive, and given his fame, ability and charisma it is difficult to conjure a vision of David living in solitude, abandoned by all. At low tide in his young life David escaped Saul and went to a cave in Adullam, near his own father's property:

"And everyone that was in distress, and everyone that was in debt, and everyone that was discontented, gathered themselves unto him; and he became a captain over them: and there were with him about four hundred men."

Now, in southern Judah, David was at the head of a formidable force of men, and how easy it could have been for Jonathan to bid farewell to his deranged father's house and join his dear friend and the future king. But he did not. Remaining true to David's friendship he also remained loyal to his father and King. We only hope that young David appreciated such a friend because his friend's father neither appreciated him nor comprehended Jonathan's greatness.

The precipitous decline of Saul as a man and a king was accompanied by his similar deterioration as a father. As a younger man there is much to admire in Saul. At first, he was lacking in kingly ambition and wanted not the crown. His manner was modest, and his natural inclinations appeared generous. Further, for a king he lived modestly and unlike his successors David and especially Solomon created neither a luxurious and lavish court nor did he indulge himself with a harem of women. Still, when Saul began his descent it was swift and with his collapse as king and man came the calamity of his fatherhood. Although he had other children our eyes have been on only two. Saul's treatment of Michal unfortunately is consistent with the attitude many men, kings or paupers, then or now, have had towards women since the dawn of creation. Michal was utilized as a game piece, her youth and likely beauty given to David not for love but as a maneuver in Saul's contest against the young usurper. Without entering the tangled thickets of modern political and cultural discourse suffice it to say that women as property is not a belief that ceased with King Saul.

A statement with a lengthy pedigree is that sometimes parents do not deserve the children that are theirs. Almost always it is expressed with the negative connotations falling squarely on the shoulders of the son or daughter. Much wisdom and truth in this observation is demonstrated generation upon generation, as the tireless efforts of good parents are trampled by the lives of bad children. Yet rarely is the reverse observed; however, we have just pondered such a case. Saul was a father who did not deserve a son with the character and goodness of Jonathan. Generous, loyal, self-effacing and without a trace of vindictiveness Jonathan still stands among the giants of the Bible. For all Saul's faults Jonathan loved his father, and with death came great poignancy. At the end of his reign, Saul, who "...had fought (valiantly) against all his enemies on every side" was defeated by the Philistines at Mount Gilboa. Now hopeless, Saul perished after arranging his own battlefield suicide. Among those killed in action that sad day was Jonathan, a steadfast son to his dying breath.

Chapter 6

DAVID, THE DISTRACTED PARENT

The Oxford Dictionary of Current English defines, in part, the word "superlative" as follows:

"1. Of the highest quality or degree
2. Something embodying excellence; the highest form of a thing."

*T*he word could easily have been coined for David of ancient Israel. David is the man from the Old Testament for whom we have more information than any other and of whom we see as the actor in more roles than any other man. From childhood to old age we have detailed descriptions and narratives of this man as a shepherd, a son, a brother, a marksman and a musician. From his youth he developed more and greater attributes and skills, a natural aura of charisma, physical strength and beauty, courage, innate leadership skills, the heart and pen of a poet, a military and guerilla leader in the first rank of history and a loyal friend who displayed an amazing and well tested loyalty to his king. Long would be the roster of adjectives and adverbs utilized to describe and analyze his character and actions, so we for brevity's sake emphasize that he was superlative. The Biblical accounts of this individual, "...a man after God's own heart" confirm that he was well deserving of these accolades.

The stories relative to David, even with the passage of three thousand years, remain so vivid, inspiring and interesting that they have long since penetrated and embedded themselves into the collective conscience of Christendom. David's slaying of the wolf and lion in protection of the sheep with which he was charged as shepherd, his youthful selection as the next king of all Israel, his anger at the blasphemy and sacrilege of the Philistine giant and his destruction of that giant Goliath have been related that they need not be retold, but merely noted here. Yet, another facet of David's character is fully subjected to Biblical revelation, and that is the concern of our present inquiry. As great as David was in a multiplicity of diverse roles, just as extreme was his conduct in two spheres which have a timeless importance for most men, that of husband and father. Many terms may be employed to herein describe David. Often these words overlap in their application, but they must include erratic, disinterested, cruel, negligent, self-indulgent, deliberately sinful and unfortunately in summation, failure.

The Bible's chronicle of his early years reveals only a nominal amount of information concerning his domestic life, and none of it is really derogatory. He married a young woman, Michal, who at the outset loved him deeply but herself was employed by her father King Saul to destroy David. Yet David and Michal remained in apparent marital contentment even though David soon had to absent himself from Michal to become a fugitive to Saul's murderous jealousy. Although this is a study in Biblical parenting principles to really understand David as a father his relationships with women must be explored.

From the moment he stepped onto the public stage David was adored by women and girls. In an era long before modern media he was effectively a media star, with the distaff sex praising him for killing tens of thousands, whereas Saul had slain only thousands. The young David was fair, handsome, athletic and even three millennia hence his form remains celebrated as an ideal of male beauty and prowess. Yet not only did the women and girls cherish this young comely male, he reciprocated, and part of his life's story is David's feelings and desire for females, often young and beautiful. The first wife Michal has been noted, and David's flippant, even callous treatment of her was discussed in the previous chapter. As the years progressed and his existence was effectively an outlaw's life, he took other women, some to marriage and some not. Most notable was a young woman named Abigail, she "...of good understanding and of a beautiful countenance." Abigail, though, was shackled in a marriage to an older man, a churlish malcontent named Nabal, who callously and arrogantly refused to aid David, at the time a guerilla leader of four hundred fighting men. David's youthful warrior ire was aroused, and he sought to lead his soldiers in a slaughter of Nabal and his confederates.

Into this cauldron of male belligerence enters Abigail, and what an entrance she would have made. A young woman, intelligent, wise, moral, far-sighted, wealthy and to most men, most importantly, she was gorgeous. With great humbleness and dignity, she reminded David that he was to be king and that surely, he did not wish his hands and soul to be stained with the blood of Nabal. In other words, David was reminded that if you are to be a King act like a King. A peace was made between Nabal and David, but soon Nabal's "heart dropped like a stone," leaving young Abigail a widow. In this age of polygamy, Abigail's widowhood was short, for David soon took her in marriage. Of course, his love and desire for Abigail was no bar to the future King's taking other wives at the same time, women named Anihoam and Jezreel.

Except as mothers of David's children none of these women plays any more than a minor role, sometimes not even that, in the remainder of the Old Testament chronicle. This is also inclusive of the numerous young women who became David's concubines (in more modern terms, kept mistresses). Neither wife nor concubine are ever mentioned as being loved by David. David definitely enjoyed women for their obvious attributes and took as many as he could, some in today's parlance might have been designated "trophy wives." The times, though, were about to change.

The story of the Bible's most famous "sex scandal," that of David and Bathsheba has been told and retold so often as to bear no repetition here except in truncated form. The King, comfortably settled into middle age, looked out from his palace one evening and saw a beautiful young woman bathing herself on an adjoining rooftop. His lustful heart demanded satisfaction, she was summoned, and their tryst resulted in Bathsheba's pregnancy. What followed was a sickening plunge into a cesspool of lying, intrigue, adultery, murder and David's temporary abandonment of monarchial responsibilities. A scheming conspiracy led to David's murder of Uriah, Bathsheba's husband and one of the best officers in David's army, an army locked in battle with the Ammonites. David now took Bathsheba, a woman we are told that he truly loved, and she bore him a son. Yet, "... the thing that David had done displeased the Lord."

In a scene with greater drama and pathos which even Shakespeare penned the prophet Nathan confronts David with his sins and pronounces God's terrible judgment upon the anointed king. First, the son which Bathsheba bore would lose his life, causing great grief. David's sins, though committed secretly, would be repaid openly by God. No, Nathan assured him, he would not die, although his conduct merited death. Instead,

> "The sword shall never depart from thine house...
> I will raise up evil against thee out of thine own

house...and I will take thy wives before thine eyes,
and give them unto thy neighbor..."

All this is the backdrop for David's career as a father. To this
point David's life accomplishments had been great, rising from obscurity in the sheep fold to the throne of Israel. Truly by labor, love
and divine gifts he had united the twelve tribes of Jacob unto one
United Kingdom of Israel. In every undertaking he proved himself
a virtuoso and doubtless men sought to emulate him, and women
adored him. God's wisdom in early selecting a shepherd boy to be
Israel's second King and father was fully proven. All families, then
and now, in whatever culture must have certain traits and conditions. One of the most important is a quality that David could not
supply either as a husband and father, and that was stability. His
younger life, much of which circumstances forced upon him, was
a long-term struggle for survival. He was literally forced to live on
the run from Saul and certain death. During these many years it
is common to say that he took many wives. More accurately would
it be said, though, that he took many women, and doubtless some
were taken for the sole reason certain men have always procured
feminine companionship, that is for physical comfort and pleasure.

David's greatness as a King was besmirched by his conduct, yet
he never lost God's blessing; however, it is as a man that his character was scarred. The sword which the prophet Nathan promised would plunge into David's heart and soul, and for his sins
as husband and especially as father he would pay dearly, deeply
and often. That first payment was made when the son of David
and Bathsheba, a baby conceived in infamy, perished. The grief
which David suffered was chronicled by the man himself in the
Book of Psalms, but it was only an initial payment before the
sword plunged again, this time even deeper into David's heart.

David's oldest son was named Amnon, and his mother was one
of David's earlier wives, Ahinoam. He has no background or back

story and is known Biblically for one ghastly, putrid act of behavior. Amnon became enamored with a young girl, and his passionate desire for her reached uncontrollable levels. Of course, this is no case of first impression and in its basic form is merely a statement of how the world and romance works. The distinctive nature of this desire, though, lies in the identity of Amnon's beloved. Her name was Tamar, the daughter of a woman named Maacah and her father being a man named... David. In other words, Amnon felt not just affection but a blazing sexual desire for his own half-sister, a desire for which he had no intention of overcoming by any self-discipline. One thousand years hence Christ Himself cautioned that the heart's illicit desire leads to illicit action, which itself is the pathway to human catastrophe. Amnon effectively had cast the die with his unbridled desire and set in motion a series of events which eventually left much of David's family in shambles.

Amnon suffered a severe case of love sickness, even to the degree of his moping and downcast behavior being noticed by his good friend Jonadab, to whom Amnon confided his great love for his half-sister, whose relationship barred Amnon from fulfilling his desire. Jonadab, "a very subtle man" was precisely the sort of man upon whom the weak lean and by whom they are easily manipulated and destroyed. Amnon's friend devised a plan by which Amnon would feign sickness, take to his bed and call for Tamar to come and feed him. Into this scheme Amnon and Jonadab incorporated David himself, who summoned daughter Tamar to go to Amnon's bedside and nurture him.

Dutifully, Tamar departed to Amnon's bedchamber and made bread in his sight. His moment at last having arrived he sent all attendants away, leaving him alone with the succulent Tamar. He took her and petitioned her to lie with him; Tamar, however, possessed no desire for Amnon, but rather she was guided by morality and common sense. She pleaded with Amnon, reminding him that such incestuous "...folly... was not in Israel." The prince, heir to the throne, answered Tamar by slamming her onto the bed and raping her. Whatever morality and emotions Amnon possessed now must have risen in his soul and engulfed him. His emotional engine was suddenly placed into reverse, and he now employed force of a different sort:

> "Then Amnon hated her exceedingly; so that the
> hatred wherewith he hated her was greater than the
> love wherewith he had loved her. And Amnon said
> unto her, Arise, be gone."

Amnon had his servants literally bolt the door after her. To demonstrate contrition and mourning Tamar placed ashes on her head, tore her garments, wept and sought consolation in the arms of another brother, Absalom. One of the coolest characters in the Bible Absalom counseled his sister to stay quiet and make no trouble over the crime, all the while Absalom continued in a business-like but proper manner with his half-brother Amnon. As for the father of them all, David, "...he was very wroth" but continued the lifelong habit of detachment from his children and did nothing.

Absalom, though, as his father's son had great intelligence, cunning and a naturally duplicitous nature. He was not always what he seemed, and two years followed the rape of Tamar.

The two-year interlude complete, it was time for the periodic sheepshearing festival, an event of great importance in an ancient nation which depended upon huge flocks of sheep to drive its economy. Absalom, a great herdsman himself, invited all the King's sons and David himself to attend, but David begged off, not wanting to be a bother to his son. Absalom sought a substitute and implored David to send half-brother Amnon in David's place. At first David refused, but Absalom's persistence finally allowed Amnon to go with all the rest of David's sons.

One day, likely in the evening after a hard day's work Amnon was relaxing with wine, he was "merry" and likely drunk. Upon

Absalom's prior directives, his servants attacked Amnon, he was killed and for Absalom the outrage to his sister now been avenged.

Bad but garbled news soon reached the ears of David, news that likely would have destroyed most fathers. It was falsely reported to David that all his sons had been killed, but Jonadab, his nephew, gave him the solace that only one, Amnon, had been murdered. Real solace it was, too, for David was "...comforted concerning Amnon, seeing he was dead." David, a man so brilliant and so adept at a multitude of roles and tasks found himself in the wretched condition as a father of being comforted at a son's death. How true were Nathan's prophetic words of the sword remaining forever in his house.

Only now, though, was King David set to embark upon the greatest of his travails as a father, and the most virulent of those troubles was named Absalom. Following the killing of Amnon, Absalom with a growing number of followers fled to the land of Geshur, where he remained for three years in a self-imposed exile. The efforts of David's great general Joab and a woman named Tekoa paved the path for Absalom's return, and finally he and his father were reunited; however, this was not to be a return to the status quo.

Absalom, who had endured two years of suppressed fury over his father's failure to do anything about Tamar's rape, was in a different position than three years before, and it was a position from which Absalom's own political strength was growing. Within two years of his return any breach in the father-son relationship between David and Absalom had been mended, and all wrongs, real and perceived, had been forgiven by David. Absalom, though, was not a boy and through the years had grown into the most impressive, capable and dynamic man Israel had witnessed since the days of the youthful David himself. He possessed his father's magnetism, natural leadership abilities and personal attractiveness. The Old Testament is never penurious when it comes to descriptions of physical prowess. Joseph, Saul and David were all described as well-built, handsome young men. Beautiful is the description, of among others, women such as Sarah, Abigail, Bathsheba and Esther. But then there is Absalom:

> "But in all Israel there was none to be so much
> praised as Absalom for his beauty; from the sole of
> his foot even to the crown of his head there was no
> blemish on him."

He also enjoyed rich, thick, luxuriant hair which grew to his shoulders and which he cut only once a year. Yet Absalom's looks, and appearance served only as an outer veneer to even greater blessings of talent. It is no exaggeration to state that when Absalom played his part some three thousand years ago the world was introduced to its first modern politician. Dazzlingly handsome day after day early in the morning Absalom stood beside the city gates. When any Israelite would come to the King to receive judgment on a litigated matter, Absalom would intercept the litigant, surely impressing him with his appearance and manner and after hearing the man's case, affirm that he should receive a favorable judgement. Over and over Absalom would do this and lament that if only he were judge in Israel all would receive true justice. His public relations blitzkrieg was wildly successful, and "...so Absalom stole the hearts of the men of Israel."

Hearts and minds were not all that Absalom garnered from his efforts. Eventually and after superb planning he had gathered political and military forces of such strength that his father King David had to flee Hebron, conceding the capital city to the rebel Absalom. Now David was to be given the opportunity to do what many desire and relive the days of his youth. Yet David's youth was not necessarily desirable, for once again the older man David was a fugitive, fearing that his life would be taken by the new pretend King, Absalom. Also, once again, David began to draw followers to himself, including battle hardened veteran soldiers and the hardened even vindictive general Joab. Absalom, for all his cunning and brilliance, had made a grave mistake in freeing David from his capital city. Now Absalom had to confront a master of ancient warfare, whether conventional or guerilla. Finally, the armies of father and son met east of the Jordan River in the heavy forests of Ephraim.

The forces of Absalom were routed by Joab, and Absalom fled the battlefield riding a mule. Alas, his beautiful long hair was about to become an accessory to his death. The mule ran under trees where Absalom's tresses became entangled in branches, and the once and future King dangled there, suspended between heaven and earth. Joab, himself, who had earlier given orders not to kill Absalom drove three darts into his heart, with his soldiers finishing the kill. With Absalom's rebellion crushed, David's great began with his lament:

"O my son Absalom, my son, my son Absalom!
Would God I had died thee, O Absalom, my son, my
son."

Joab, for one, the hardened brittle soldier, was unimpressed, and he rebuked his king with the solid statement that many men had given their lives for David, yet he had grief only for his rebellious son. Yet David's grief would continue, and even after his death the sword would dwell in his household. David's oldest son Adonijah coveted the crown, but David had promised the kingship to Solomon, his son by Bathsheba. Even following David's death Adonijah continued to claim the crown, but Solomon ordered the death of his rival half-brother. For now, though, the sword promised by Nathan lay still.

Let us now pose the question that must be considered. How could a man such as David, so brilliant, so brave, so talented and in many ways so virtuous and admirable be such a failure as a father? From boyhood throughout much of his kingship David was a man of action. He fended off wild animals as a young shepherd, magnificently answered the challenge of the Philistine, slew Goliath as history's most famous underdog and performed honorably and brilliantly while a fugitive

from Saul and then as monarch of a united Israel. In so many parental crises, though, a strange hesitancy and at time paralysis overtook
him. When Tamar was the victim of incestuous rape he did nothing
for two years, all the time Absalom's rage building. Upon Absalom's
murder of the rapist Amnon, David again did nothing for three
years, and two years hence he even forgave Absalom. Even following
Absalom's rebellion, which came within a hair's breadth of success
David's usual vigor seemed to be mortgaged to his worry and grief.

Although few parents ever find themselves with royal responsibilities an experienced mother of father can easily recognize David's
dilemma. A parent, including David, is dealing with his own flesh
and blood, and he is hesitant to make a mistake. With Amnon he
could have ordered his own son's death, thus assuaging Absalom and
satisfying the law, but how many parents could order the death of
their own child? Simply stated, David, as any honest parent easily
grasps, did not know what to do, so he did nothing. David's inac-
tion is consistent with the Biblical story, for any father-child interaction with David and his children is rarely noted. Sometimes in-
action, though it may be unwise or plainly wrong, is not the same
as indifference. David certainly cared for his sons and daughters,
but the enormous pressures of his life seemed to distract and de-
ter him. Any serious father or mother can identify with this.

David's true failure as a father is directly traceable to his failure
as a husband. Even being as liberal and generous as possible in fac-
toring into the moral equation the reality that this was a polygamous
age David's marital record does not well withstand scrutiny. He took
so many wives that scholars are reluctant to assign to that group a
precise number. The number of his mistresses cannot really be esti-
mated. Again, being generous for a traditional male weakness, David
was a lustful man. When his eye caught the beauty of a woman who
stirred him he took her, and almost exclusively the unions seem to be
based solely on desire, not love. The one exception is Bathsheba for

whom David apparently had love. Yet, it is difficult to engender any sort of sentiment for a love begun in adulterous desire and resulting in the murder of a good, even noble, man. Some men have been known to express a defense for being a poor husband by some variant of "But I am a good father." A stronger position, though, may be offered by stating that the first thing a father should do is love his child's mother.

David's many children were raised in a cauldron of turbulence, half-brothers and half-sisters galore, a father often absent (though often he was blameless for this), and wife after wife added to their father's collection. The family unit did not exist. It was a collection of individuals and cliques with its patriarch continually distracted, at times with his own survival, additional women, or ruling the nation. There is no wonder that the sword never departed from David's house.

Yet in the aggregate we should be reluctant to offer too much condemnation. He was a public, Biblical and historical figure, with both his virtues and faults writ large. We should never forget, though, that a thousand years hence Jesus Christ without hesitation or shame claimed the title Son of David.

Chapter 7

NAOMI, THE REWARDED PARENT

*T*he narration of the Book of Ruth has traditionally focused upon the eponymous character Ruth and justifiably so. While the character of Naomi, essential to the story, has hardly been ignored, she has too often been relegated to the shadows. The lives of these two women become so linked and intertwined that neither can be removed from the story without a drastic loss of meaning and dramatic impact. It remains, though, that as with all humanity Naomi and Ruth were distinct individuals, with different backgrounds and stature, and therein lies much of the story. The love throughout years of almost unbearable pain and hardship and the triumph which they eventually won is a tribute to that love and the character of each woman. How often we forget, though, that stories that glow with happiness at their end often have copious amounts of travail and tragedy along the way.

During those times before the reign of kings when Israel was a theocracy ruled by judges a famine's dark destruction spread throughout the nation. All were affected, including a family which lived in an obscure village in Judah called Bethlehem. Elimelech had a wife named Naomi and two sons, Mahlon and Chilion. Before the famine they lived comfortably, perhaps even idyllically, but this pleasant existence was shattered by the famine and the sudden death of Elimelech. Now a widow with two sons and dwelling in a locale ravaged by famine for survival's sake Naomi took her two sons and immigrated to the country of Moab, east of the Jordan River and there lived for ten years.

Moab was a land where the famine's devastation was not as omnipresent as in Israel. It was a small Gentile nation, often at war with Israel, and pagan to its core. Religiously, the Moabites were quite similar to the powerful Canaanites, the original inhabitants of Israel and notorious for the vileness, baseness and brutality of their religion. Still, Naomi's sons married two young Moabite women named Orpah and Ruth. The marriages were not long, though, as Naomi's sons died, leaving a legacy of widowhood to the two Moabite women. From a pleasant life in Israel within a few years this family was reduced to three widows, destitute and facing starvation. Naomi, hearing that the famine was over, decided to return home but advised her daughters-in-law, each of whom she loved, to return to their own mother's homes. In scenes filled with emotional gloom, pathos and weeping Orpah parted from Naomi and went home; Ruth, however, received the same spur and blessing from Naomi, including a recognition that Orpah would return to paganism and Gentile ways. Ruth, though, offered a statement of such lyrical and poetic quality that it has never lost its power:

> "Entreat me not to leave thee, or return from following after thee: for whither thou goest, I will go; and where thou lodgest, I will lodge; thy people shall be my people, and thy God my God: Where thou diest I will die, and there will I be buried; the Lord do so to me, and more also, if ought but death part thee and me."

This proclamation and subsequent events would prove that biology alone does not equate to motherhood. In all things that matter Naomi and Ruth had become mother and daughter. Historically and to the present many persons, male and female, will readily recognize and rejoice at such a bonding. So, Naomi returns to Israel and specifically to Bethlehem, her home which sadly she had to leave ten years earlier; however, this was a drastically changed Naomi from the former Bethlehemite. She said to all "call me not Naomi, call me Mara" for the Almighty hath dealt very bitterly with me. The embittered woman exclaimed that she had left full, full of family, children, life and the future, but now returned "empty" and impoverished. In our despondency we are prone to exaggerate for Naomi was not totally empty. She had Ruth.

Bitter, joyous, happy, morose or whatever, all who live must eat. The Mosaical Law provided for the poor and instructed farmers that when they harvested grain from their fields, the corners were not to be reaped. The remaining grain was to be "gleaned" by the landless poor, which certainly included Naomi and Ruth. But to glean you must have access to grain, and here Naomi had resources, a kinsman of her deceased husband who was a wealthy farmer, so to those fields Ruth went to glean grain. This wealthy man, Boaz by name, noticed a young damsel gleaning grain, inquired of her and was told her story by his workers. Boaz, whose motives may not have been entirely spiritual, instructed his young workers that she was to gather as much grain as she wished and cautioned them that they were to defer to the girl and treat her respectfully. One thousand years before Christianity Boaz had essentially become history's first "Christian gentleman."

Ruth was highly successful in her gleaning tasks and returned to Naomi with both a great deal of barley and wheat and great news about finding favor with the esteemed and wealthy Boaz. As developments will soon reflect the tumblers were clicking in Naomi's mind, and she likely instantly grasped an exit strategy from their present poverty. Meanwhile, she counseled Ruth, continue to glean in the rich grain fields of your kinsman Boaz. Gleaning and winnowing grain made for survival, little more, so Naomi both saw and devised a solution to the women's peril.

It is often stated and expressed in so many ways, many worn by usage to the level of clichés, that difficult circumstances reveal character. That of both Naomi and Ruth has been intensely tested so far, but the testing period is hardly over. Naomi is opportunistic, not necessarily in any nefarious manner, but in seeing the chance to make the most of situations. From either a cursory or thorough review we see that Naomi possesses few apparent assets. She has no money, no men in her family and seemingly is bereft of manners in which she may improve the situation of her small family. Naomi realizes that the greatest asset she may claim is her young widowed daughter Ruth, and she has designed means to utilize that to the fullest extent.

The short Old Testament book of Ruth from which we get our story provides no physical description of its namesake. Whether she was fair and beautiful or plain is a subject of silence, but Naomi sensed that to Boaz at least Ruth was attractive and enticing. Also, of paramount importance is the kinship of Boaz to Naomi, for Boaz was more than just a wealthy neighbor who had shown a spark of interest in Ruth. The Mosaical covenant required that a man was obliged to marry his brother's widow so that the family name might live through the propagation of children. "Brother" in this matter was apparently being interpreted to include other male relatives and kinsmen.

Naomi is proof that while character is the quality of the greatest importance knowledge of the facts and of human nature is not to be disregarded. She knew from experience and years of living what is still of prime importance in the relationship between women and men. In a maternal manner she instructed Ruth to wash, wear perfume and dress in your best clothes. While Naomi is hardly preparing her daughter to be a seductress she wanted it a certainty that Ruth appeared as desirable as possible. Further, Naomi knew that as the day neared evening Boaz and his workers would be on the threshing floor where they would be winnowing the chaff from the grain. At the end of the work customarily the men relaxed with eating and drinking, perhaps even drinking wine just a bit to excess. Ruth was counseled by Naomi to go where Boaz and the other men were working and then relaxing, but initially not to make her presence known to anyone there.

Here let us remind ourselves that this is an ancient rigidly patriarchal society where women traditionally were highly reticent about any activity that could even be conceived as "forward" behavior. Even in these post sexual revolution days of twenty-first century America in many, if still not most, sectors of society too much obvious and aggressive feminine behavior is not favored. Social mores and customs, be they ancient or modern, often fall by the wayside when desire and necessity intensify. Naomi's wish and desire, and it was intense, was that Ruth marry Boaz so that they all could have some sort of a future and for Ruth, happiness.

As she was bid by Naomi, Ruth followed instructions and went to the threshing floor after Boaz had lay down for the night's sleep. Softly and gently she came to him and lay down at his feet. The apparent effrontery of Ruth's actions even three millennia hence, is still worthy of note. Boaz's reaction to all this is quite normal for any culture in any age. It was after midnight when he suddenly awoke to find a young woman in his bed, and he stammered out an inquiry regarding her identity. Ruth, well primed to answer, immediately exclaims that she is his kinsman and "... therefore, spread your shirt over thine handmaid; for thou art a near kinsman." In our simpler modern terms, she is simply petitioning him for marriage because of the dictates of the Law of Moses.

It must be recognized that a threshing floor bed at midnight is a bit of a curiosity as a forum for discussing nuptials between a man and a woman who hardly know each other. Yet Boaz did know of Ruth by brief observation of her hard work and exemplary loyalty to her mother-in-law Naomi. Shaking away the stupor of heavy sleep his conversation proved that he had already acquired a detailed and admiring knowledge of Ruth. Boaz commended her for her steadfast loyalty to her mother-in-law when she could otherwise have made herself available to young men, be they rich or poor. All of the townspeople of Bethlehem already know of your goodness, and I, Boaz, will gladly perform the "obligation" of a kinsman and marry you. This desired marriage, though, has an impending roadblock, perhaps an insurmountable obstacle, of which you are unaware, Ruth. Boaz then explains that although he is a relative, he is not the nearest relative, an honor that belongs to another man, who has precedence over me. Boaz, though, did assure Ruth that he would marry her should the other kinsman decline.

So, Ruth returned home to Naomi, not yet with the prize of marriage but a consolation prize of more grain and still the plausible hope of marriage with Boaz. Naomi seemed satisfied and cautioned Ruth to be patient because "... my daughter... Boaz will not be in rest until he has finished the thing this day." Thus, Naomi fulfilled a role known by mothers throughout history in cautioning their children to be patient.

Not only was Boaz a man of his word, a near relative and honorable but he also proved to be a man of action. In ancient Israel it was common for business to be conducted openly at the city gates, and those gates of Bethlehem soon were host to Boaz, and negotiations began when this man, forever unnamed to history, came by. So that whatever be the outcome was public and known to all he had ten of the city elders sit at the conference. According to the strict terms of the Law for this man to obtain Ruth he also had to purchase, or "redeem" a piece of land which Naomi's husband Elimelech had owned and which was now owned by Naomi. The man, though, possessed a keen knowledge of the Law, and said that if he redeemed Naomi's property and Ruth's hand in marriage he would "... mar mine own inheritance." Our nameless stranger, who played a role of substance in history thus waived his rights, which now acceded to Boaz. Now, the triumphant Boaz proclaimed to the elders and to all the townspeople:

> "Ye are witnesses this day, that I have bought all
> that was Elimelech's, and all that was Chilion's and
> Mahlon's...Moreover Ruth the Moabite, have I pur-
> chased to be my wife."

Modern western civilization is repelled by the concept of arranged marriages, marriages of obligation or purchased marriages, yet this was not so with ancient cultures. Naomi's reaction to Boaz taking Ruth was historically exuberant as she exclaimed:

> "Blessed be the Lord, which hath not left thee
> without a kinsman, that his name may be famous
> in Israel."

She happily continued and saw Boaz as a "...restorer of the life, and a nourisher of thine old age." Yet it was for her beloved Ruth that Naomi reserved her highest praise and accolades, for she was a woman better than seven sons. It is not surprising that Naomi would employ the number seven, a Hebrew symbol of completeness and perfection, in describing Ruth. Surely, she forever missed her deceased sons, but with Ruth she had established a mother daughter relationship replete with all its elemental virtues save biology.

A common cliché fashioned to describe a life of ups and downs is that a person has been on a rollercoaster ride, a term which would have given pause to an Israelite of the Old Testament. Some may even be tempted to apply this to Naomi, but it would be patently incorrect. Established in Bethlehem with a husband, a home, property and the promise of a rewarding future her life instead became a series of plummets from precipices. Likely she looked forward to a life of settled pleasure with a husband, two sons and doubtless many grandchildren, but the vicissitudes of real life, often terrible in their manner and even more in their consequences, began to ravage her. Famine, death, widowhood, homelessness and more became Naomi's bitter life. Through death and the inevitable hardships of life Naomi was rendered destitute and abandoned. How easy was it for her to see that she had no hope and no future joys and blessings. By the grace of God, though, one asset only remained to her, but it proved to be the one essentiality, a remarkable young woman in Ruth. This was a person who though raised in pagan idolatry apparently had an even greater appreciation of Naomi's God than did Naomi herself, and she elected to follow Him rather than return to her homeland's Canaanite practices.

Sometime, somewhere at some unknown and perhaps unknown moment the relationship of Naomi and Ruth transcended its in-law status and effectively became mother and child, a bond that is and always has been prevalent in all cultures. This is natural, in layman's terms biologically encoded into the genetics of the mother, but it is not foolproof. Some women, hopefully still a minority, are at best uninterested or indifferent to their own children and in more extreme instances both hateful and harmful. This is counterbalanced, though, by the large number of women who become mothers by desire rather than solely by reproduction. Even those of us who may never have been partakers in such bonds may view with sympathy, good will and admiration those who adopt children, the good among foster parents and the numberless emotional bondings that are witnessed with women and various relatives and even non-relatives. The maternal instinct truly can be awesome in its power, but the love of the adopted (whether legal or otherwise) son or daughter is just as potent. So it was with Ruth.

How dreadful and awful it must be to live an existence of bitterness and assumed hopelessness, where even the good, bright memories of earlier happier days now are daggers of torment to the heart. So it was with Naomi, for she surely accepted that her good days were gone, family, prosperity, happiness, laughter and all the good that is attendant. Now she concedes that she would more rightly called Mara, or "bitter." Ruth was God's ray of light which penetrated and began to illuminate the darkness of Naomi's days. Ruth – and Boaz. Together both were the restorers of Naomi's life and soul. Her life now transcended its past miseries, as she went from loss, heartache and despair to the rewards of respect, a daughter "worth more than seven sons" and a son-in-law who merits the title of "great men" more than many who are given it.

All parents, even the best and those who have the best children realize that parenthood entails a lifetime's hard work and worry, patience, drudgery, disappointment and heartache. To lose sons early as did Naomi compounds all these dismal factors, and the death of those sons and subsequent loss of one daughter-in-law precluded them from ever being a source of joy. Yet Naomi ultimately was rewarded, and the reward was great, for its source and conduit was Ruth, an exceptional daughter, doubtless an exceptional wife and probably an exemplary mother. The days of Naomi's bitterness ended, and her life was undoubtedly lived with pride and respect.

So what of Ruth? This story has long been proclaimed and idealized as one of the great love stories of history. Further, Ruth's statement of her love and loyalty to Naomi to this day is held as a benchmark of the best of human qualities. Still is this all it really is, a nice love story with a happy ending? Certainly, but Ruth's love and loyalty cast a long shadow. She and Boaz had children, and one of her great-grandchildren became the second most famous man from Bethlehem. King David's fame was exceeded only by Bethlehem's most famous son, a descendant of David and Ruth, the true Redeemer, Jesus Christ.

James Kifer

Chapter 8

Mary and Joseph - Amazing Normality

*F*or thousands of years Galilee had no particular significance. In Old Testament days it was the northern district of Israel, or Palestine, and for much of its history contained no defined geographical boundaries. When the Israelites evicted the Canaanite residents from the land that would become Israel and began settling this new Promised Land its northern sectors were taken by three of the more obscure tribes, those of Zebulun, Issachar and Asher. In its long struggle with the Canaanites these tribes were not completely successful in ridding the land of its pagan natives, and in Old Testament times the Galilean area retained a Gentile hue to its culture. Naturally, intermarriage occurred between the remaining Canaanites and the Galileans, resulting in many indicia that marked them as somewhat different than their southern brothers and sisters.

Most importantly Gentile idolatry had a strong grip on the northernmost Jews, the Galileans, and they eventually succumbed entirely to paganism, being among the Israelites that were carried away to Assyrian captivity in the eighth century B.C. and to be lost to the Jewish heritage forever. When the remnants of the Jews returned several centuries later a portion of them settled in Galilee, but it was a Galilee separated from the main line of the nation in the south, Judah, by the mixed-race province of Samaria, where the residents were intermixed Jews and Gentiles, usually scorned by both.

Galilee ("district" in Hebrew) continued as Jewish, but to some degree it developed separately from Judah. These were now the years of the rise of the Hellenic, or Greek culture, a powerful force that exuded a huge pull on all nations, Galilee, though, more than Judah. Later, of course, came the western influence of the first century B.C. Romans. The net effect of this history was to make a Galilean Jew somewhat distinct from his brother, a southern Jew. He spoke with a pronounced accent, usually derided as crude or "country" by his more sophisticated Judean friends, and Galilee itself, geographically cut off from the capital of Jerusalem was perceived as a cultural backwater. It is difficult not to recognize that by the first century AD to the mainstream of the Jews in Judea the Galileans were poor country bumpkins and rednecks. Further, we have to admit that there existed some historical justification for these attitudes. The Old Testament, among other things, is the most detailed ancient historical account of any one people, the Jews. Yet those same scriptures only rarely mention Galilee or its inhabitants, with center stage almost always be allotted to the south. Once again, though, the Divine eye was proven not to be identical to the human, and in this most unlikely and even mocked region everything was about to change forever.

One a day otherwise of no special importance the angel Gabriel appeared to a young girl in the nondescript Galilean village of Nazareth and proclaimed:

> "Hail, thou that are highly favored, the Lord is with
> thee: blessed art thou among women.And, behold,
> thou shalt conceive in thy womb, and bring forth
> a son, and shalt call his name Jesus....And of his
> Kingdom there shall be no end."

The girl, Mary, was of no fame, no pretense and no apparent pedigree except that she was from the lineage of David. At first frightened and bewildered she was calmed by the angel and assured that although she was a virgin the baby's conception would be from the Holy Spirit. Thus began what was and will ever be the most famous and told story of history, the birth of the Son of God to an unknown girl from a town held to be contemptible even by other Galileans.

God in His wisdom had selected Mary to bear and to raise His only Son, yet His wisdom in parental matters was to be further demonstrated. Mary was currently betrothed to Joseph, a carpenter in this same town, and in accordance with custom they were to be married within that betrothal year. He was now confronted with a dilemma of singular difficulty, for no other young man has ever faced such a conflicted situation. Joseph is engaged to a girl who claims that she is a virgin and yet she is the bearer of an ever-growing pregnancy. His own doubts of Mary's story must have been real for his first impulse was to divorce his espoused bride. Surely, Mary had succumbed to another man, and in ancient Jewish first century life, a society of strict sexual mores, this could be more than a private matter. It could be considered as a crime warranting severe punishment. Should Joseph turn on his own beloved Mary and accuse her of taking another man he might be condemning her to an early death. Should the two of them continue in the engagement all the townspeople would assume, yes even "know" that the two of them had sinned before marriage. It was a monumental burden placed on a young man such as Joseph, but his God was the same as Mary's. Strength and understanding were imparted to Joseph when an angel appeared to him with words he must have cherished that "... he fear not to take unto thee Mary thy wife."

So, the engagement, the marriage and most importantly the birth of the Savior would proceed, yet Mary and Joseph would still endure the scorn, the hateful looks and perhaps even ribald jokes regarding her early pregnancy. Yet God found in a Galilean teenage girl and a young carpenter the faith and strength as parents which would ever be tested. The next great test would be the almost one-hundred-mile journey to Bethlehem over rough roads, harsh conditions and Mary's having to endure the difficult burdens of a late term pregnancy. This story, told, retold, filmed, celebrated and reenacted countless times we know as the Christmas Story. Told so often we will not indulge in another retelling other than to note both Joseph and Mary bore the severe strains and pressures magnificently. They were now the parents of a newborn with all the work and worry that entails. Yet there was more.

Herod the Great, aged but as powerful, jealous and vitriolic as ever was still king. Having heard of the impending birth of a Bethlehemite baby who would be the true Eternal King he ordered his soldiers to kill every male child two years or younger in Bethlehem and its vicinity in the historically infamous "Slaughter of the Innocents." To thwart the malevolence of one of history's most notorious villains again an angel appeared to Joseph and directed him to remove his young wife and baby to Egypt where they would be safe. Again, the burdens of a long, arduous journey befall Mary and Joseph, but yet they complied. They lived in this foreign land until Jesus was five, and they returned to Nazareth. Before they left for Egypt, though, one unique encounter with an elderly man foretold to Mary her life as a mother.

In Jerusalem lived a man named Simeon, and to him God had promised that he would not see death until he had first seen Christ. As was dictated by law and custom Mary and Joseph brought their new baby to the temple in Jerusalem, to which Simeon had been led by God. He held the baby, blessed Him and gently said:

> "Lord, now lettest thou thy servant depart in
> peace...For mine eyes have seen thy salvation."

Simeon then turned to Mary and praised what her son would be, but also warned "...a sword shall pierce through thy own soul also." It will be no surprise to any mother or father that parenthood has access to a plentiful reservoir of heartache and pain, but the sword which pierced Mary's heart would be different than any other. Even the parents of the best children have not raised perfect men and women, but Mary was to see her perfect child, the only such child, taunted, mocked, subjected to unspeakable cruelty, called blasphemous names and suffer the perfect injustice of the ignominious death of a criminal. For now, though, these matters lay in the future. She had a baby to nurture and a child to raise.

From those days of infancy to age thirty when He began His public ministry the gospels contain only one story about Jesus, a story that likely reveals as much about His parents as it does about Jesus Himself. The Passover time of year arrived when all Jews went to Jerusalem to offer sacrifice. Joseph's family, traveling in a caravan of neighbors and relatives made the journey and soon after began the long trip back to Nazareth. A day's journey had elapsed, but the twelve-year-old Jesus was nowhere to be found. As rapidly as ancient travel would allow they returned to Jerusalem, where He was found three days later. The youth was back in the temple discussing religious doctrine and matters of the Law with learned teachers, amazing them with His knowledge and understanding. His once panic-stricken mother rebuked Him for causing His parents such grief and anxiety, but He readily replied:

> "...wist ye not that I must be about my Father's
> business."

Yes, Mary and Joseph were grateful to have found their son safe, but "...they understood not the saying which he spoke unto them." This incident and the exchange between parents and son begs two questions to be examined. First, what was and how extensive was the understanding of Mary and Joseph as to the nature of the son to whom they had been entrusted? Each had received God's promise and prophecy through angelic revelation, yet in the plainest terms we must ask what did they really know and understand about their eldest son. We are further compelled to wonder about the knowledge and understanding of Jesus, son of Joseph and Mary. A Christian has no hesitancy in accepting and believing that the thirty-year old man knew in His foreordained manner that He was both the Son of God and the Son of Man. But did the five-year old Jesus understand this, and just how thorough and deep was the intellectual and spiritual grasp of the twelve-year old youth?

Regarding the extent, depth and time of Jesus's realization of His full identity and character that is a question the answer for which is vouched safe only in the minds of the Father and Son. It may be asserted, though, that as with the maturing of the years customarily comes a growth in understanding, including self-awareness. It was after the temple incident that the winter Luke remarked:

> "And Jesus increased in wisdom and stature, and in
> favor with God and man."

Certainly, Christ's knowledge and wisdom were living things and continually growing. As with any of us the five-year-old, the twelve-year-old and the thirty-year-old were different persons. This is a subject of ceaseless interest and fascination. In keeping with the parental theme, though, it is that initial question which here should be our concern. Mary and Joseph, as human as any of us, were not possessed of Divine insight, and they had to make their way through the thickets of parenthood just as all others do. Jesus was their child and their charge, and God had ordained that for a few brief years He would be subordinate to them. A central question remains, however, and that concerns what they could teach the Son of God. Whatever and however they proceeded their works and methods were marvelously effective, as the gospel writer Luke confirmed. With these brief incidents we have exhausted our reservoir of Biblical examples, so we must think and speculate. Joseph and Mary, two apparently ordinary persons performing ordinary tasks and leading ordinary lives had as a child, and their first child at that, the Son of God.

What could they teach and what could Jesus possibly learn from them? Some matters and lessons are so obvious that they do not require speculative thought. Joseph and Mary were both devout Jews, doubtless well instructed in the Mosaical Law, and with certainty these lessons were passed to Jesus and later his siblings. So well, in fact, that this same Jesus as an adult continually thwarted the intellectual designs of the scribes and Pharisees to trap him. The heart and soul of the Law was not the rules and regulations of the Levitical priesthood nor the fine points of tithing but rather the basic moral precepts that are the superstructure for any worthy society yet today. The tenets of honesty, sobriety, commitment, loyalty to the right things and persons and the underlying spirituality of life were doubtless taught from the cradle. Surely, though, all good Jewish parents taught these matters, as do all decent parents ever since. Was there something, some lesson or lessons that Mary and Joseph gave to Jesus that were unique to this parent/child relationship?

One of the oldest maxims, one that has been expressed in an endless variety of ways is that "I would rather see a sermon than hear one any day." Although teaching, especially including parental teaching, is vital to the spread of Christianity this adage, simple as it is, permeates the scriptures. Teaching by human example, whether good or bad, shall always be a powerful, dynamic force. May we not ponder that the greatest teaching that Joseph and Mary offered was the ever-present instruction of their lives' examples. This is really not hard to consider for this is universally true for almost all families. All families, though, do not have divinely selected parents and a child who is both the Son of God and the Son of Man. Jesus, even as a child, was special and his knowledge and awareness of all matters was necessarily special as well. From His own innate Divinity and early teaching, He knew that all humanity lives under the cloud and the curse of death. Leading to that dread moment were two God ordained curses, one upon men and the other upon women. To find that curse upon men we reach all the way back to Genesis, where God told the fallen Adam:

> "In the sweat of thy face shalt thou eat bread, till
> thou return unto the ground; for out of it wast thou
> taken: for dust thou art, and unto dust shalt thou
> return."

From that point man has had to toil to even survive, and it was an understanding given to Jesus at a very young age. His father Joseph was a carpenter, an occupation easily understood and comprehended in all ages and cultures. We must be reminded, though, of what carpentry really meant in an ancient first century setting. The raw material of wood had to be hewn by hand from trees. All tools were primitive, made by hand, and likely in many cases by the hands of the carpenter himself. Precision measuring devices, glues, solvents, varnishes and all manner of construction aids belonged to the future, and for now all was the work and effort of the skilled artisan. These were only the physical labors, though.

Jesus saw his father work many days when work was the last thing with which Joseph wished to occupy himself. He witnessed Joseph working day upon endless day in hard, exacting labor, but likewise never saw his father fail in his responsibilities to his family. As with any trade or business carpentry was surely not one long upward trek, where everyday business was better and better. Jesus saw his father worry when business was poor or even non-existent. He saw Joseph battle frustration, anxiety and perhaps even anger when customers did not pay bills in a timely fashion. How could his father deal with all this, including the occasional difficult and over-demanding customer, day to day for a seemingly endless eon of time, Jesus must have wondered. Then he thought of his mother Mary as he observed her.

Likewise, Mary endured her curse begotten by the Fall:

"I will greatly multiply thy sorrow and thy conception; in sorrow shalt thou bring forth children..."

Mary is the most honored mother in history; however, the honors came not without costs and payment. Jesus was the first child of
Mary and Joseph, followed by four brothers and at least two sisters,
but still only one mother. It can be imagined, discussed and written about, but is it possible in our more comfortable modern age to
truly recognize and comprehend the nature of motherhood to seven
children in ancient times? In an obscure village in a hot climate with
no cooling devices whatsoever the mother of the Savior awoke early,
likely before dawn, to commence a day of labor. She prepared meals,
likely had to daily carry water into her home, self-prepared almost
everything that was done daily, cooking, cleaning and taking care
of children. Hopefully and prayerfully they were healthy sons and
daughters, but even so they would need constant and changing types
of care and nurture as they matured. The physical demands of motherhood were so exhausting, but perhaps the mental and emotional
were greater. No good mother has ever failed to lose sleep over her
child and the child's problems, be they health, fears or an endless array
of situations for which the mother has no readily discernible answer.
The best children themselves are hardly carefree and the family relationships test the wisdom of any parent. Jesus, as any maturing child,
surely saw the heavy, ceaseless demands upon his mother, Mary.

The young Christ saw great virtue and goodness in both Mary
and Joseph and it is a certainty that they taught Him well, even brilliantly, by both word and deed. Still for all the goodness and good
works in all the days of their lives, for all the travails and tragedies
Christ knew where their lives would end in death. The terrible curse
brought into the world by the Fall hangs heavily over every living creature, and especially men and women, for we know that we are going

to die. Surely the Son of God learned these lessons as His parents taught Him daily by their living examples. Where did all the character and virtue of responsible, kind persons such as His mother lead but to the grave? Death was a curse, and its effects could be removed by only one person, Christ Himself. He knew and explained that it was for this mission and reason that He came into the world. Only the son of Mary and Joseph could remove the pain of their deaths.

A Christian has no doubts that Christ was sustained throughout the terror of His Passion by the sustenance and strength given Him by His Heavenly Father. He bore it because God granted Him the extraordinary Divine strength to bear all the sins of the world through pain, agony and degradation. Throughout those horrors which began in Gethsemane, that moment when he was arrested, dragged before High Priests, Herod Antipas and Pontius Pilate, He said little but must have been thinking much. As He bore the heavy cross on the Way of Sorrows enroute to Calvary He spoke to weeping women, warning them of the times of Roman destruction and desolation which were in their future. Then on the terrible cross for but a few hours He spoke several times, and all but one statement showed His concern not for Himself but for others, especially his mother. Through the torrents of pain and maelstrom of agonies surely, He consoled Himself with the Heaven soon to come. The whole ordeal, however, also had a very personal facet which we must remember. Jesus knew that just as the sword of the Roman centurion would pierce His side so also would old Simeon's prophecy to Mary be fulfilled as a sword would pierce her soul.

All the Old Testament prophecies were fulfilled, and Christ triumphed on the Sunday following this Good Friday when He rose from the grave. Yet it was a quiet resurrection, seen first by Mary Magdalene and then by a few more disciples. The second triumph will not be as quiet, though, as the son of Man will descend in all His glory, taking to Him his beloved followers. As His great apostle Paul queried:

"O death, where is thy sting? O grave, where is thy
victory?"

His greatness shall be revealed fully then, and the curse finally
eradicated. It had all begun some thirty-three years earlier, again
quietly, unobtrusively at His birth to a remarkable young couple,
unfamed and still not even today full appreciated, Mary and Joseph.

Chapter 9

HEROD AND HERODIAS, THE HORROR

*I*n the world's long history of state sponsored murder, violence, waste, buffoonery, chicanery and all other manner of vices and evils it is doubtful that few, if any families, equal that of the Herodians, a large clan whose time upon history's stage, coincided with the centuries immediately before and after the birth of Christ. The Herodians produced an assortment of kings, governors, tetrarchs and miscellaneous rulers, with royal feet in both the western and eastern worlds. It was a family that was basically Edomite (descendants of the Esau of Old Testament fame) with an ample mixture of Jewishness added. They ruled over the Jews, sometimes all the Jews but more often only a portion, basically pretended, with no real enthusiasm or commitment Judaism itself, but were kept in power only by the discretion and pleasure of their masters, the Romans. In the matter of having buildings, various edifices and monuments constructed they met with a large degree of success, but most of these structures have long vanished or lie in ruins. The real legacy of this family is its gross immorality, lying, murdering and incest.

The first of the family to emerge from the backdrop of history was a man named Antipater, who was appointed by the Romans to be governor of Idumea in 67 BC. It was Antipater's second son, our first Herod, who introduces the family to the larger stages of the world and the New Testament. This individual, known to his contemporaries and to us as Herod the Great has for two thousand years remained the most infamous figure in the Herodian family history. Herod became governor of Galilee in 47 BC, just three years prior to the assassination of Julius Caesar in Rome. Although just twenty-five years old at the time he now began a long career of climbing the political ladder, murdering many of his own wives and sons in the process, and constantly ingratiating himself with the highest ruling powers in Rome. In 41 BC Mark Antony, along with Octavius Caesar, one of the two successors to Julius Caesar, added the tetrarchy of Judea to his realm.

Above all else, Herod the Great was a political chameleon and acrobat, as accomplished in those enclaves as any man our world has ever seen. The sharing of power in Rome between Antony and Octavius was not fated to last, and soon the Roman realm began to divide into two factions. At first Herod had the favor of both Antony and Octavius, but as hostilities between these two became open, Herod initially opted for Antony; however, it was Antony who was vanquished by Octavius's forces at the Battle of Actium in 31 BC, leaving Octavius (soon to be rechristened the Emperor Augustus) as the sole ruler of the Roman world and Herod on the losing side of the political fence. With his consummate political skills and highly developed absence of morals he quickly ingratiated himself to the new emperor and solidified not only his position as King of all the Jews but also as ruler of many additional provinces which Augustus assigned to him.

Much of all this has been outside the direct scope of the Bible, and important though it is for Biblical purposes, the legacy of Herod the Great finds its focus in two items of historical value. Herod, of course, was the author of the Slaughter of the Innocents, his decree that all male babies of the vicinity of Bethlehem be put to the sword so that the promised (and to Herod, feared) Savior would be eliminated literally in the crib. The second and most pertinent is that he fathered Herod Antipas, whose actions perhaps are the most influential of any of the Herod family in the New Testament. At the death of his father Herod Antipas (hereafter "Herod" or "Antipas") became the ruler of the province of Galilee, home of Jesus of Nazareth.

Herod Antipas, while not quite as successful or powerful as his father, proved to be a worthy successor and was just as slitheringly serpentine as Herod the Great. Early in adulthood he married a woman whose name is lost to history, but who was the daughter of a Gentile King. Circa AD 29 Herod made a trip to the west to consult with his Roman masters, and enroute stopped to visit his half-brother, Herod Philip, who evidently lived in one of the coastal cities of Palestine. A fateful visit this would be, not only for the Herod family but for the soon to be founded Christian religion. Herod Antipas became enamored with a woman named Herodias, who happened to be Herod Philip's wife and thus the sister-in-law of Antipas. This is in no event surprising due to the seemingly inborn character of the Herods and also due to Herodias being described by contemporary historians as beautiful. Yet Antipas, ruler of the Jews, already had a wife, and among the Jewish people the days of polygamy had become an historical relic best left deep in the Old Testament. In any event, the marriage to Herodias would be unlawful under the Law of Moses, which prohibited marriage to a brother's wife (except for the levirate exception discussed in Chapter Six). The Romans, especially the upper and certainly the ruling classes, had a casualness, at times bordering on flippancy, towards marriage and divorce which moderns would easily recognize. Thus, throwing law, caution and morality to the winds Antipas and Herodias agreed to marry as soon as Antipas returned from his planned trip to Rome. Not without political repercussions was this divorce and marriage to Herodias, but with these we will not presently concern ourselves.

The bluebloods of Rome may have had an easy going, even dilettantish attitude towards divorce and re-marriage, but not the Jews, particularly one Jew. He was the son of Zaccarias and Elizabeth and the second cousin of Jesus of Nazareth and known to all as John the Baptist. The final and greatest prophet of Christ, John had a faith and value system as different from Herod and Herodias as was possible. He had come to prepare the way for Christ and salvation and make "straightway the paths." John preached with the stark directness of many of the Old Testament prophets, especially Elijah, and his message of redemption and coming salvation stirred the populace. For a brief period before the public ministry of Christ he essentially served as both a prophet and the moral conscience of the nation. This young prophet succinctly and tersely stated to Herod:

"It is not lawful for thee to have her."

Herod Antipas, although only partially a Jew ethnically and only a nominal one religiously was a Jew nonetheless, a man familiar with the Jew's laws and religion, which to Gentiles, including Romans, were absurd and weird. Herodias, though, was married to Herod Antipas, a ruler of Jews, and this is likely the extent of her attachment and likely her understanding of Judaism. Now the teachings of God through His prophet John and the family, life and parenting skills of Herod Antipas and Herodias are set for a collision.

To Herodias, the Roman sophisticate, John the Baptist must have seemed a crude, backwater preacher, a "lower" class Galilean who had the audacity to criticize and interfere with the life she had staked out for herself. As an individual, though, Herodias possessed no independent political, military or civil powers. Her status was the wife of the tetrarch of Galilee, yet she was far from powerless.

The force which Herodias could summon was feminine sexuality and sensuousness, which has proven itself through time immemorial to be capable of literally changing kingdoms and moving empires. At least in this instance it was more than sufficient to move Antipas to action. Apparently for himself Herod Antipas had adopted a "Live and Let Live" stance towards John the Baptist. Likely he had become accustomed to the "ravings" of seemingly mad Jewish prophets, and their words had a minimal effect upon him. Herod, though, had his set of fears, and they included large numbers of Jewish subjects, many of whom listened to John's teachings and likely knew the illegality of Herod's marriage. In Biblical terms "... he feared the multitude." Likely his more immediate fear was found in his own marriage bed, for Herodias hated John the Baptist, so much so that Herod "... put (John) in prison for Herodias' sake." Whether Herodias employed rage, threats or her own likely not inconsiderable feminine charms with her husband she had succeeded in throwing into a dark prison the one innocent man in these proceedings. It is likely that she employed a combination of her talents, demonstrating that if Herod ruled Galilee, Herodias ruled Herod.

The opportunity of a lifetime now came to Herodias. She must have felt that whatever heathen gods she prayed to had smiled favorably upon her. Still, it was an opportunity which success required innate intelligence, cunning and guile, careful planning and a moral heart as black as midnight. It also required the participation of the daughter of Herodias, an apparently seductive young beauty. Fortunately for Herodias's designs she was abundantly supplied with all these qualities.

Of all things the great opportunity came in the form of a birthday party, a birthday party for her husband, Herod Antipas. Both Testaments of the Bible frequently record the ceremonies and parties of the high and the mighty, and the "great and the good." This likely was done because of their ubiquitous nature and the opportunities they provided the monarchs and all rulers to demonstrate their conviviality and, underlying it all, their power. The gospel writer Mark informs us that Antipas was in the midst of military commanders, high officials in his government and perhaps even a representative or two from Rome. Again, although it is unstated, it is almost impossible to imagine the staging of such a social occasion without the free flow of abundant streams of alcohol. Further, a really good party requires entertainment, and this was to be this highlight of the evening. Herodias had a young daughter, unnamed in the Bible, but known to us from the Jewish historian Josephus as Salome. She, of course, was the stepdaughter of Herod Antipas, but she was also a blood relation being the daughter of Herod's brother Philip. Thus, she was both the stepdaughter and niece of Herod Antipas.

Salome, a name which has become synonymous historically with seductress, danced for Herod and his friends, and she received rave reviews from Herod. The Bible does not specifically identify the nature of the dance, although it is unlikely to have been classical ballet or a charming folk dance. Whether correct or not it has been historically known and mythologized as the "Dance of the Seven Veils" and forever cemented securely the image of Salome as the young seductive siren. Whatever it was this scene has been immortalized in countless paintings, stories and motion pictures to the present day. It also succeeded well with Herod. Herod Antipas, the stepfather and uncle of Salome, a man himself in later middle age sat there with his like-minded colleagues drooling and salivating over the charms of his own niece and daughter. Oh, was Herod swept away for:

> "He swore unto her, whatsoever thou shalt ask
> of me, I will give it thee, unto the half of my
> Kingdom."

The desires and plans of Herodias, who would have earlier killed John the Baptist were tumbling into place with the perfection of precision. Salome consulted her mother as to what she should request of Herod, and Herodias pronounced those immortal words:

> "The head of John the Baptist."

Straightaway Salome went to Herod and made the request for John's head "... in a charger." Herod, again playing his customary role of a craven coward, but because he had sworn an oath and also not wanting to look "bad" before his friends, acceded to Salome's wishes and ordered the beheading of John the Baptist. As requested his severed head was placed in the charger, which Salome then dutifully delivered to her mother Herodias.

Everything fell into place perfectly in the plan of Herodias, and characters were revealed in the harsh glare of reality. John the Baptist likely lost his life to the blade of an axe, but the real murder weapon was Salome. Herodias had plunged into the depths of an immoral abyss as is seldom found. That a mother would literally employ her own daughter, her physical charms and sexual allure to kill a man is repugnant to any standards of decency and morality. The beauty and desirability which were Salome's were not evils in themselves, and in fact were God given. Sensuality in women is divinely ordained and of itself is pure. To enlist it, however, and in the form of your own daughter was to convert Salome into an agent of murder, just as certainly as a knife or a gun. It has never been uncommon for certain parents to recruit their own sons and daughters for diabolical means. This work has previously noted the manner in which King Saul employed his son Jonathan and daughter Michal in attempts to destroy David. Throughout most nations divorce courts are the tribunals in which every conceivable battle is waged fiercely, and in which the custody and support of children form the primary stock of ammunition. Herodias was a horrible mother, an unfaithful wife to her first husband and a cold-blooded murderer. Effectively she became the Jezebel of the New Testament.

What of Salome? In this story Salome, for all her undoubted charms, was an obedient servile lackey. The standard Hollywood pitch of this story would likely show a very young (and very attractive) Salome as simply little more than a child, pressed into service by a devious mother and salacious stepfather. We, however, do not know Salome's age, whether it be fifteen of twenty-five or something else. Salome may not have had the corrupted heart of her mother, but she was of age and knew what she was doing. We daresay that most girls and young women know the effects which their persons may have upon the male gender. Thankfully, most have some sense of decency and propriety, and but a mere few would contribute to a murder plot. Salome is never again mentioned either in the Bible or in historical chronicles, so hopefully we can place some trust in the fact that most men and women mature morally as they age and that such activities did not continue to define her character.

The conceptions and images of fatherhood have been evolving steadily and in various ways since the patriarchal days of the Old Testament. Little agreement, at times even among Christians, is to be found in the definition of fatherhood. Yet, except for the most extreme modernistic radicals, one point of agreement is that a good father exhibits strength. By this measure alone Herod Antipas, tetrarch of Galilee, was a wretched failure as a ruler, a father and a man. His life was an almost endless series of survival, self-promotion and advancement by always taking the course of least resistance. He possessed more than a modicum of power, which the Romans allowed him, but he possessed another character trait that permeated his moral fiber and defined him, the trait of cowardice. Likely Herod was physically a coward, but even worse he was a moral coward.

Herod survived a childhood and youth as the son of Herod the Great, no mean feat itself, where he likely developed an especially keen sense of the desirability of his own survival. His illegal and immoral marriage to his own cousin, Herodias, placed him squarely in the crosshairs of Bible history and of John the Baptist. Herodias outraged at John's teachings desired his death. She was without power on her own, except for the power over an exceptionally weak husband and governor, and she thus secured John's imprisonment. Herod, known that John was "… a just man and holy" nonetheless meekly acquiesced to the vicious demands of Herodias. Here, as both a husband and a ruler he was found wanting, being unable to stand up to his wife's illegal demands. The writer Mark tells us that while in prison John the Baptist gained the ear and perhaps even the friendship of Herod, who enjoyed talking with him. It was to no avail, though, when Herod's birthday arrived on the calendar, and he had his great birthday banquet. He sinks even further into moral depravity when with a type of weird ghoulishness, he is enticed by the provocative dancing of his own stepdaughter and niece. When Herodias demands the death of John the Baptist, Herod's cowardice plummets to rare depths. Again, he cannot stand up to her murderous desires and is afraid of the disapprobation of his powerful friends at the banquet. The result is the death of a great and an innocent man. In the New Testament drama, though, Herod Antipas was assigned one more scene to play.

When Christ was brought before the Judean governor Pontius Pilate, who wanted no part in these proceedings, as a true politician Pilate sent Jesus to Herod, tetrarch of Galilee, in hopes that he would handle the case of Jesus of Nazareth, a Galilean Himself. With the backing of "his men of war" Herod arrayed Him a gorgeous robe, mocked Him and returned Christ to Pilate. Once again, Herod the "fox" as Christ Himself had called him cowardly evaded responsibility.

No story, and certainly no life, is complete without its ending, so we ask what of Herod Antipas and Herodias? These benchmarks of immorality and parental degeneracy continued in Galilee for a few years more, but the political winds in Rome began gusting and blowing in a new direction. Both Herod and Herodias traveled to Rome where Herod sought from the new emperor, the insane Caligula, the title of King.

Unfortunately for Herod Antipas, he was not the only Herod. Herod Agrippa I, the nephew of Antipas, convinced Caligula that Antipas was corrupt and acting contrary to Rome's best interests. Instead of the glory of a King's title Herod, accompanied by Herodias, was banished to Gaul (now France), where presumably they died forgotten and in obscurity. Two Millenia later, though, they emit a toxic radiance of horrible parenthood.

As for the innocent victim, John the Baptist?

From Christ Himself:

> "Among those that are born of women there is not a
> greater prophet than John the Baptist."

Chapter 10

THE GRIEVING PARENTS

*P*arenthood is grief. Yes, it is so many other things, from the excited anticipation of the birth of a baby, to the satisfaction of the child's attaining and passing various milestones on the path of life. When the baby first walks, begins to communicate by speaking intelligible words and begins the process of learning and education, both formal and informal. With keen interest and hopefully delight the mother and father witness the child slowly develop his or her own personality, see the child learn and develop interests, make friends and in general just become his or her own person. The fortunate parent revels in the recognition of the child by others, sometimes even "officially" by school, church or other organizational awards. Most importantly the father or mother reaps the benefits of parenthood when scenes of developing moral character are played out in front of them, and the parent can experience the satisfaction of having helped in the development of a morally productive person of whom anyone would be proud.

All of this is the bright shiny side of the parental coin; however, from the beginning the Bible was never reluctant to show the sorrows, tears and frustrations of parenthood. The abyss and depression into which a mother or father may find themselves is never hidden or reserved in tacit silence. To the best parents their children's lives will deal them a full hand of pain, disappointment and hurt feelings, and to the worst moral and emotional agonies we all wish to avoid.

All parents, good, bad or indifferent, share several points of common experience. Their children are seen sick, injured and in pain. In these modern times much of this may be mitigated by medicine and medical technique. In days heretofore much pain and sickness, about which a suffering parent could do nothing, simply had to be endured as part of life. None of this has yet to even touch upon those matters which potentially and, in fact, usually cause greater sorrow and grief than matters in the physical realm. Yet, one grief is paramount above all others, one is a sword, which pierces the heart of a mother and father and at times effectively destroys. This, of course, is the early, premature death of a child.

Truly, the death of a child is an experience which must be personally borne to be fully understood and appreciated. Unfortunately, our world has been home to a substantial body of humanity which has shared in this trauma. Before the advent of modern twentieth and twenty-first century society, the stillborn baby was likely a part of most families' histories. Further, the early deaths of children from a variety of reasons, including untreated illness, wounds and the rapid spread of communicable disease was a fact of existence. Of course, such conditions are not unknown in many portions of the world today.

The death of a child likely is the hardest of all deaths to accept, for it seemingly upends the order of the universe. It is the way of the world and God's own order that our parents are usually fated to precede us in death. Almost all understood this, and though there may be grief, its sharpest pangs abate, and we go forward. With brothers and sisters, we accept that some leave this life before others, and though causes sadness it is borne. Certainly, the death of a husband or wife, and the resulting widowhood and often loneliness may be emotionally cataclysmic. Even here, though, except in the rarest of instances one spouse dies prior to the other, and it is generally accepted. A parent must feel a victim of some celestial crime or disorder when a child is taken prematurely. It is remarkable how quickly the Holy Bible addresses the issue of such parental suffering.

The Genesis story of Cain and Abel had always been related as the first murder, when the elder Cain killed the younger Abel in a moment of jealous rage. Of a piece with this, though, it is also the story of the first loss of a child, and how much more intense the suffering of Adam and Eve caused by the murder of one some by the other. Further, their grief was compounded by the estrangement of Cain as a "fugitive and a vagabond in the earth." Nothing could assuage the grief of Adam and Eve for they had lost both sons. Although more children were to come could there ever be comfort and real solace to Adam and Eve for having to part with both sons?

Centuries later Isaac and Rebekah almost saw and experienced the identical grief with their sons Jacob and Esau. Following the breach between their two sons Jacob escaped to another land to avoid a murder of revenge by his own brother. As if the aging father and mother Isaac and Rebekah had not suffered enough from their child, Esau continued his profligate "wild child" way which was "... a grief of mind unto Isaac and unto Rebekah." The later in life reconciliation of Jacob and Esau could not have removed the years of grief and suffering endured by their parents.

As instructive as are these stories of grief it is in the New Testament where the true suffering and parental grief is found, but here is also found the personal touch of Christ and later His Comforter. Jesus lived in a time like ours, but again not like ours. For much of history, and in ancient times death was more omnipresent, a spectre of which all were aware, as it would come as suddenly as a fatal untreatable illness. Today, as much as possible, death is hidden. Whether the deceased expires at home, a hospital or elsewhere the body is taken immediately to a funeral home where it is prepared, behind closed doors, for funeral services and interment. Increasingly, bodies are no longer publicly displayed for viewing. Doubtless, people in the twenty-first century grieve for family and friends just as much as did their ancestors two thousand years ago, but the process and result of death is more veiled.

Christ, the Conqueror of Death, was never afraid nor hesitant in confronting it. The writer Matthew records an event wherein most observers assumed that Jesus arrived on the scene too late to fight the all-consuming clutches of death. A ruler of the synagogue, a man named Jairus, petitioned Jesus that He should come and save his twelve-year-old daughter, who lay dying of a fever. Upon arriving at Jairus's house Christ cleared the room of all its many mourners. Before they left, though, they laughed Christ to scorn when He told all that the girl was only sleeping, not dead. Now in the room with the girl remained only Jesus, the apostles Peter, James and John and her parents. He bid her "arise" and so she did to the astonishment of her parents. The counsel of the scornful mourners was obliterated, but Christ cautioned all to "...tell no man what was done," a ringing refutation of all supposed faith healers who publicly glory in their presumed "powers."

To underscore the public acknowledgment and treatment of death in New Testament days we look at another incident which occurred in the small village of Nain. Christ came upon a funeral procession wherein the only son of a widow was being carried out, presumably for burial. No thinking, decent person needs special instruction in the difficulties of widowhood, but perhaps we need to be reminded from time to time. Not only does this woman suffer emotionally with the absence of her life's partner, but also economically her position is now tenuous. Her first line of support would naturally be her children, but now her son, her only son was gone. As the bier was carried it is no shock that the woman was grief stricken and weeping. For her motherhood was now to be accorded a morose even despairing taint with the pride and comfort of a son gone forever.

The happiness gathered from memories of motherhood were likely to be poisoned now with the grief of remembrance, and most certainly for her parenthood now equated with grief. The good Shepherd, though, witnessed all this and knew even more, as "He had compassion upon her," and the son rose from the dead at the Master's command. When he arose, the young man began speaking and Christ delivered him to his mother. From such vignettes as these, sparsely worded, do we learn much of the nature, personality and character of Christ. The woman and her deceased son must have been well liked as a great number of mourners had followed them out of the village. Here Christ seemed to take notice of a large public audience, and so performed the miracle of resurrection before many; however, when the daughter of Jairus was raised the act was intentionally secreted from public view and those who did witness it were told to say nothing. Christ did not act in the same manner in similar situations and really only He knows His reasons for his comportment at all times. For our purposes, though, we can easily grasp a common theme in these miracles. Only Christ cannot only mollify pain and grief, but He can literally turn grief into joy. In the purest sense Jesus brought parent and child together again, as He literally reconciled them.

The times of the earthly miracles of resurrection are recorded in the scriptures and in the hearts and minds of believers, but they are no longer of a current existence. Christ personally walks with us no more, and the days of the apostles are two millennia past. To the believing Christian, though, even today only Christ can make the unbearable burden of loss through death bearable, and only He can offer succor and solace from the other griefs of parenthood. This is perhaps best and most clearly illustrated by an incident recorded by all three of the synoptic gospel writers. Demonstrated here is that death is far from the only source of severe parental grief, and that grief is certainly not confined to believers only.

One day Jesus was surrounded by an enormous multitude, a diverse group which included His disciples, His detractors, and likely the largest element, those that had come to benefit from His miracles. Out of this horde of humanity Christ selected one man, a father who then presented his petition. I have a son, he explained, in the most pitiable position imaginable. At times a spirit overtakes him, throws him to the ground, and he begins writhing in agony, gnashing his teeth and foaming at the mouth. Many have presumed that the man was graphically describing an epileptic seizure, but whatever the nature of the condition the father lamented to Christ that His own disciples were able to do nothing for his son. The father has described the moment which among the most dreaded for parents, that of witnessing a child in sickness, pain and distress and being unable to do anything. It is grief in one of its purest forms. Here Christ, too, was grieved, for he lamented the inability and lack of faith with which His own ordained apostles were hamstrung. So, the man's son was brought to Christ, brought to the one whose touch, whose word alone, could alter any, even the most desperate, situation. When the young man came to Christ all present witnessed the full horrors to which he was subjected. He tore loose from his escorts, again fell on the ground, piteously rolling about even into a fury, and foaming at the mouth. "Have compassion" and "help us" implored the boy's father.

Christ, though, did not immediately offer help, but rather asked the father a question, a question which was in the form of a declaration:

> "If thou canst believe, all things are
> possible to him that believeth."

The man responded with simple words, but words with which all believers and even seeking non-believers grasp in a moment:

> "Lord, I believe; help thou mine unbelief."

How thoroughly and succinctly does that capture the belief/disbelief dichotomy found in all disciples! In a given situation, a long-standing problem, a riddle seemingly with no solution the committed disciple has faith, the faith that "... all things work together for good to them that love God." Yet somewhere in both the mind and the heart is that nagging doubt that this time the problem will not work itself out, that this problem is too rooted and too entangled with no apparent solution. The believer says, as did this father, yes Lord, I have a long and strong faith in you, but I really do not see how You can cut this Gordian Knot and make everything straight and right again. The father was a good man and a good father, but he was one of us, with his similarly being borne of the grief and fears we all share.

Christ charged the evil flee from the young man and so it did and with such violence the crowd assumed he was dead. Not so, for Christ took him by the hand, and once again restored or reconciled son to father. It is the truly rare person, the rare mother and father who has not asked from an abyss of despondency "Will this situation ever improve?" Sometimes, maybe even say often, they never get better, and any mature realistic adult knows this, and in such cases the grief of the parent grows and intensifies. In plain vernacular, the bad situation may grow worse, and certainly the Bible is not remiss in offering such examples. Yet the parent's grief is if anything greater, and a famous Old Testament story illustrates this worthily.

The difficulties which attended the fatherhood of King David were discussed at some length in Chapter Six, but we shall make one extended reference to them here. We recall Absalom as the brilliant son of David, and as a man who seemingly had no limitation to his gifts and talents. Enraged by his father's indolence in not punishing his half-brother Amnon for the rape of his sister Tamar, Absalom became duplicitous and turned against his father. By virtue of abundant political gifts, personal attractiveness and charisma he turned much of the population against David and ran his father and father's government into the wilderness. David was now presented with the grotesque, even macabre, duty of waging a civil war against his own son. David's army was triumphant, and Absalom was killed, bringing David not relief but rather regret and remorse over the life of a beloved son. His extended grief is historical, even legendary, but most cogently it was real. Surely David did not mourn the murderer Absalom. He mourned his son Absalom. The good in his son's life, the destroyed talents, the wasted years of David's fatherhood and more now and forever would torment David. The grief was so deep and extended that David's general Joab harshly criticized the King for his prolonged mourning. Where now were David's joys and pride of fatherhood? Gone and gone from this life forever, and that, too, meant grief for the pain would not be alleviated. David knew that the death of a child was not the worst pain a father could endure. It was the death of an estranged son, a son who had grown to hate him, that was now his benchmark of grief. For an indeterminate sentence of years David would live with the agonies of grief, the paroxysms of guilt and the dark knowledge that he could never make things better and right with his son Absalom.

A poet once mused that nothing is so sad as unrequited love, but he was wrong. As sad and heart-wrenching as is a love given but not returned is a grief which is unending. Without indulging in triteness or banality the mature man or woman, mother or father, recognizes that some problems in the parent-child relationship are highly unlikely to be either resolved or even improved. They must be "lived with" and accepted as a part of life. Yet acceptance and acquiescence in the darkness of grief is fundamentally at odds with the Christian ethic. Is there a way to reconcile these two opposites, grief with joy and despair with hope? The only conceivable answer to this must come from the great Agent of Reconciliation, Jesus Christ.

On the night before His crucifixion Christ was surrounded amidst a group of very confused and distraught men, His own apostles. He knew the fear that began to grow in them when He told the men that His time with them was short. Three years of living and walking with the Son of God were ending, and they would be alone. But no, not really alone for He promised that:

> "...the Father... shall give you another Comforter,
> that He may abide with you forever."

Thus, the promise of what we know as the indwelling of the Holy Spirit was made not to the apostles alone, but to all Christians. Christian parents are not excluded from its breadth. For two thousand years so much has been written, said, taught and preached about the Holy Spirit, and much of it is nonsense. In the end His comforting presence may really be felt, and His healing touch welcomed but not understood. We accept the mysterious gift as we accept much on faith, but a faith constantly sustained and proven. It is this Spirit that lights the candle in our darkest gloom and guides us through the valley of the shadow of death. God never promised that every moment of parental life would be joyous, and He never promised that all gloom and despair and the despondency of hopelessness would lift in a moment. But He did promise His followers that He would never abandon them in the thick of the fight.

Again, who can explain how God really works in our lives, but He does and certainly not just through the indwelling of the Holy Spirit. No being has ever had more names and titles than does Jesus, and among the most glorious is that of Intercessor. Two thousand years have elapsed since Jesus walked in Galilee and Jerusalem, yet "... He ever liveth to make intercession..." As a mother or father who is grieving over the fate or even the loss of a child the parent desperately looks for help. When all sources of help are apparently exhausted, when all the solutions have been tried and failed, all thoughts are of despair and all tears have been shed, and all the grieving mother or father can manage is to sit and stare blankly into space, Christ is still there, still at the right hand of God and still making intercession. Now or perhaps later the intercession will prove successful, for in the penultimate chapter of the Bible He declares

"Behold, I make all things new."

Chapter 11

LOIS AND EUNICE: THE OVERLOOKED MOTHERS

Sitting in a dank, gloomy Roman prison cell late in the 60's AD and awaiting the executioner's axe the apostle Paul penned his final New Testament words to his protégé Timothy. Early in this letter, which would become known to the world as the book of II Timothy Paul makes a brief reference to two persons whose names appear nowhere else in the scriptures:

> "I (am) filled with joy, when I call to remembrance
> the unfeigned faith that is in thee, which dwelt first
> in thy grandmother Lois and thy mother Eunice;
> and I am persuaded that in thee also."

Those few words are the Biblical Alpha and Omega for these two women, for they appear neither before nor after. Beyond a few brief references to times and places we are on unstable footing if we try to author a biography of their lives. Of their lives, yes, but perhaps in these few unadorned words from the apostle a biography of character may be constructed, not only for Lois and Eunice, but of countless mothers past and present which stories have never been told or explored.

No one could rightfully deny that motherhood itself has not been the subject of intense historical and literary interest. The stories, books, poems, motion pictures, television shows and legendary recounting of mothers and motherhood are so vast that they can be neither categorized nor catalogued. Traditionally, in different manners perhaps, but in most cultures, motherhood has in some fashion been exalted and idealized, but in reality, there may exist a dearth of examination and analysis of what it is in light of the Biblical ideals of motherhood. By word and example, though, the Bible is not lacking in its exposition and spiritual idealization of motherhood. This is easily viewed in the prominence of place the Bible gives to Jochebed, the mother of Moses, Rebecca, Elizabeth, the mother of John the Baptist and the most famous of all, Mary, the mother of Jesus. Their stories have been told endlessly and forever they deserve the retelling, yet what can we learn about motherhood solely from a brief reference to Lois and Eunice?

They were woman of faith and the two were among the earliest Christians, providing the lineage, care and moral instruction to one of the early church's greatest leaders, Timothy. "Faith" is itself a world of lessons, teachings, parables, morality plays and issues which discussion resists a swift brief encapsulation in a small essay such as this. Suffice it to say that it is a large section of the bedrock foundation of discipleship to God. In Paul's sentence description of Lois and Eunice "faith" does not stand alone, but is modified by the adjective "unfeigned," a word far less familiar to us and not in the common speech of very many persons. Effectively it is a religious faith which is unpretentious, unstimulated and without wavering. In short it is the faith that throughout the scriptures and the ages has been held up as the purest form of faith, the one to be desired. In the plainest terms it is the real thing. A Biblical incident is recalled when we think of "unfeigned" faith. This is the faith which Christ saw and commended in Nathanael when He greeted him with "Behold an

Israelite in whom there is no guile." It is the purest faith in the purest form and found in consistently the most faithful of all followers, the dedicated mother. It is the faith not only of Lois and Eunice nor even Mary, but the faith of the unselfish mother even today.

What are the origins of this unfeigned faith, the pure faith and love for which this commendation is made? It is impossible to separate faith from love, just as it is impossible to separate Christ as the highest and purest definition of all things good. Unfeigned faith is a composite virtue, composed of many factors, but with three in particular which stand out above the others.

The first of these is subordination, and it was demonstrated in its highest form by the Son of God coming to earth and living as the Son of Man. He lived a simple, though at times harsh life, with humiliation, criticism, indignities and hatred which no other man has ever endured. Yet again in the words of Paul "...Christ made Himself of no reputation, and took upon Him the form of a servant, and was made in the likeness of man." From the majesty of the right hand of God on His Throne in Heaven He willingly subordinated His glory and royalty to live humbly and to be as we are, to be human.

A sacrificial death was the essence of Christ's life on earth, and the element of sacrifice is essential to a Christian. He willingly walked the road to Calvary and bore the sins of all for our redemption. Yet, He was not so required, for He assured His apostles, who heard in wonderment that:

> "... I lay down my life, that I might take it again. No
> man taketh it from me, but I lay it down of myself. I
> have power to lay it down, and I have power to take
> it again."

In plain words He endured the most painful and sacrificial of deaths because He so desired to suffer to redeem His "sheep." It is difficult to imagine any gospel scene where Jesus was taking from others. So giving was the Master that on the cross itself six statements of His are recorded, and all but one is concerned with the welfare of other persons, even those who drove the nails into His hands and feet.

Indispensable to unfeigned faith is the element of service, which is the heart and soul of Christian discipleship. Once again, the entire life of Christ is a demonstration of service. Only a few hours before His (not the apostles) crucifixion He humbly washed the feet of His apostles, an indicia of the most menial form of service. He provided the living embodiment of the principle of Christian services, that the greatest Christian is he who is the greatest servant.

Subordination, sacrifice and service, a trinity of traits which defined "unfeigned faith" has attained its apogee and quintessence in the person of Jesus Christ. May we speculate as to where among men and woman it is most highly developed and manifests itself to the greatest degree? The greatest realization of unfeigned faith is found in the good mother, of whom Lois and Eunice are named, but also of whom countless exemplars to the present day are to be found. Historically young girls and women have desired children and have sought at least partial fulfillment in motherhood. Some have not for many reasons and have wisely elected to forego this type of responsibility. For this decision they should be accepted and even commended for their self-awareness. Now, though, we focus on the unfeigned love and we may say the unfeigned desire of young women for motherhood. The young Christian woman is desirous of a lifelong commitment that in so many fashions is emulative of the sacrifice and love of Christ Himself. In seeking self-fulfillment consciously or not her spirit of motherhood is that of seeking her true self in the fulfillment of another person, her child.

As with all the young, the mother-to-be is not fully aware of the burdens that accompany the satisfactions of motherhood, and yet so many bear them, and the best do so in a magnificent, exemplary fashion. It is so easy and even cliched to remark that motherhood requires total commitment, but not even the best, the most ideal, of mothers has the totality of her time to devote to being a mother. This is not so because of her lack of desire, but rather because of the reality of the human experience. To her has been allotted the responsibility of nurturing, loving, tending and protecting a helpless infant recently arrived in the world. To her has also been assigned the duties of managing a household, caring for and tending a husband (who at times may be more infantile than the baby), looking after the health and well-being, physical and emotional of all family members and quite often in the modern age the responsibility of work and a career outside the home. To manage all these tasks and burdens she is also assigned the same twenty-four hours a day as is every other woman and man.

Let us examine the object of the young mother's attention and affection, the newborn child who accompanies the mother on her return from the hospital. That infant is the celebrity and immediate star of almost every gathering, whether it be family, church, work or other association, and both men and women are rivals in competition to proclaim the infant the sweetest, cutest, prettiest, etc., that their eyes have ever beheld. The baby is almost always what they proclaim, and the adjectives innocent, enchanting and adorable may be tossed in for good measure. Yet that is not the complete description of any infant that has yet to be borne. They also are selfish, demanding, self-centered, merciless and in modern parlance, gross. No baby has yet arrived who is considerate of other's feelings, especially these of the mother. The baby never reasons that "Mom has had a bad day, so I will let up and be easy on her." Mothers know that the opposite is much more likely to be true.

Even the healthiest baby demands continual attention, nursing and nurturing, and obviously some more than others. Our protagonists, Lois and Eunice likely knew this with a son such as Timothy, a man for all his virtues apparently was a sickly nature. Even his mentor Paul counseled Timothy to:

"... use a little wine for thy stomach's sake,
and thine often infirmities."

As with most, Timothy's poor health likely began in child-hood. Even the healthy child offers time and labor demands to the mother, and what is worse worry. Continual trips to the doctor's office, even emergency room visits and in more severe, intense cases, hospitals themselves, lay burgeoning, wearying and worrisome burdens upon the mother. By the time an infant and then a child has grown to adulthood the mother may rightfully view herself as a composite figure of a doctor, nurse, pharmacist, health care specialist and health insurance professional.

The years of infancy and babyhood, however demanding, pass with a startling swiftness. The mother's demands may modify, in some instances cease, but others rise to assume their rightful places. Medical appointments may become less frequent and the physical demands of caring for children less onerous, but the demands of motherhood have now been transferred to different areas. School activities, parent-teacher conferences, sports events and church youth activities grow in frequency and importance to the child. Almost everything demands money and additional portions of the mother's time, and the whole scene can become a seemingly endless ordeal. While the demands increase the importance of peers, of friends, reaches giant proportions as the child "matures" into the teen years. Now, though, in addition to changing and shifting burdens there also appears a shifting family dynamic. As friends, perhaps especially with daughters, become increasingly important the mother may sense that the demands on her time and psyche have in no way diminished, yet she senses a slide into a secondary role in her child's esteem and affection. A moment with her child, an afternoon social event or event time alone in conservation, all of which were once esteemed by both mother and teen are now seen as a ritualistic boring obligation to the child.

Even in view of all the labor, obligations, worries and even conflicts the mother-child relationship invariably survives the demands of infancy and childhood and even the trauma of the teen years. In fact, the older mother, likely remembers the rapidity and quickness with which these periods flashed into view but then vanished.

So, with the child or children adult, mature and in some manner at least "on their own" is the mother's role finished and may she even rest on her laurels? If she so chooses she may, but the good, conscientious mother never retires or even relaxes from her role. She may find pride in a job well done, glow at her child's accomplishments, moral strength and bright future. Just as likely, though, she may have herself placed in the most difficult, worrisome and frightening period not only of her parenting tenure, but also of her life. The good mother will have raised her child with a strong moral foundation and structure and will also have attempted to infuse into her son or daughter the capacity to be independent and think for themselves. Worthy endeavors all, but what if these principles now become poles of conflict in her own child? For example, what if she has raised a son, now a grown young man, intelligent, attractive and ready to strike out on his own? In his self-view he may have "mastered" the independence aspect of adulthood, but now much of his moral training he may look upon as unnecessary superfluous baggage which must be jettisoned as soon as possible. She deals with problems as they now arise, and she reaches into her reservoir of parental authority and control and now finds very little or nothing.

The mother of the adult son or daughter retains all the feeling, love, other emotions, worry and fretfulness which she has always possessed, but she is now lacking the vital element of control. In the worst of situations, she may be forced to view her son embarking upon a path that will lead to his destruction, but she has no real way of stopping him. Even her influence and advice may be continually rejected to the point where she senses that her son is rejecting her very character as a mother. As the son's path of self-destruction widens and lengthens the first glints of doubt and self-recrimination begin to appear, and she wonders whether all those years of love, pure unfeigned love, sacrifice and service were given for naught. To add to her mental anguish is the dawning realization that this may never end, the son may not return, and she must re-examine her beliefs and motives. He may be in close physical proximity to his mother, but he remains as far from her as possible. Yet life continues and so must the relationship between parent and child and upon the most pleasant level as possible. As will be examined in the following chapter a son or daughter can remain at home and also remain "prodigal." The daily repetitive pace of life proceeds, and outwardly everything seems as fine as ever.

As Christ said of the scribes and Pharisees so it may now be said of the feelings the son has for his mother:

"(They) honoreth me with their lips; but
their heart is far from me."

The mother worries, prays, endures sleepless nights, stands unseen vigils on her son's soul, and the son and his situation remain stagnant. Hopefully, though, a moment comes, without fanfare or dramatics, when the son's heart, head and attitude begin to change slowly and even imperceptibly, and a lifetime's worth of moral teaching and life's advice begins to faintly reappear in the son's thinking. Often it is not accompanied with any drama whatsoever but rather a slow (and at times even unadmitted) awareness that his life has been "going nowhere" and that his partial rejection of moral teaching has hastened failure down the road. The change in the son is not always and necessarily visible at first, but the slow accretion and accumulation of sound and virtuous thinking and living begins to carry the day. His life glimpsed at any one moment may not necessarily appear to be special and certainly not spectacular, but the son is on the road home. Whether he is consciously aware of his altered thinking and life (and doubtless he is) his path and direction modified he must be given credit for a change of heart and life. But are all the honors to be given solely to him? For a proper and thorough answer to this question a return to the opening of this chapter must be made.

Unfeigned faith is the substance of Paul's great commendation to two women, Lois and Eunice, a grandmother and mother who raised Timothy and produced a splendid man, a giant figure in the early Church. The mother of the son in the present story possesses the same unfeigned faith and love, yet her rewards of satisfaction and pride in her work are slower to mature and ripen. She knows that unfeigned love is not short-term nor is it even long-term, but rather this love is for life. The rains come, the winds blow, and even the foundation itself may shake, but the structure of love of which she has been the family architect stands. She in her unfeigned love is the temporal embodiment of the eloquent Paul's great definition of love, especially that which recognizes that love:

> "Beareth all things, believeth all things,
> hopeth all things, endureth all things."

But perhaps the greatest aspect of her love is her essential unawareness of its depth and its brightness in a dark world. When her son began his journey back to his heritage and home he was walking towards the Light, the Light that is in Christ but also the light that is his mother's life and teachings. When Christ told His disciples that they were the "light of the world" surely in the fore of His thoughts was His own mother Mary and those whose lives have replicated hers. The mother is in the forefront of those described by Christ who on the Judgment Day are bewildered when Jesus commends them for tending to the poor, the sick and the imprisoned Savior. She is astounded that Jesus would so praise her, and she responds that she never did it, that she has never even seen the Savior until this moment. Christ's words in response will be inspirational to His followers, His sheep, until that day He returns:

> "Inasmuch as ye have done it unto one of the least
> of these my brethren, ye have done it unto me."

When the mother was sick and sleepless with worry over the state of her son in a far-away place she touched the figure of Christ as he worries for His sheep. When she despaired that her son would never again appear at the welcoming hearth of home she approached the agonies the Savior knows over the hopelessly lost. As tears well in her eyes and streamed down her face she approached the suffering Savior who still cries for the lost. As with Lois and Eunice her unfeigned faith and love is a model and a rock. Assuredly she will be among the first to hear these glorious words from the Master:

> "Come, ye blessed of my Father, inherit the
> kingdom prepared for you from the
> foundation of the world."

> Chapter 12

Gains and Loses

The story has been told and retold, examined and re-examined so many times and in so many ways for two thousand years that even the strongest disciple may question whether anything is to be gained by revisiting its narrative. Even though it has often been called the single greatest piece of literature ever crafted is there any moral lesson or treasure yet to be mined from its rich seams? Actually, the succinct answer to this question is yes. As the apostle Paul once recorded this story's depths and riches are fathomless, for in a brief scenario and the employment of a few hauntingly moving sentences Christ paints a picture of family life and relationships that spans time, generations, races and cultures and draws characters with whom all can identify. It has been called by many titles but most frequently is it known as the Parable of the Prodigal Son.

A very wealthy father evidently possessed much land and controlled a fair amount of wealth, most notably in the persons of his two sons, the younger of which had reached the end of his patience, often a patience of very short duration with young men. The younger son, though, possessed two qualities that often are discovered in great abundance in young men, the desire to be independent and "on his own" and the burning desire to be free of any restraints, especially those of his father, to whom he now goes with a demand, a demand met by his father. The youth wants his inheritance now, and his father offers no resistance. Without compulsion of any sort the father divides the inheritance between both his sons. If he acted in accordance with Jewish law and custom the elder brother received twice the share of the younger. Nonetheless to the young man he had received enough so off he went free at last.

He went far from home and with money in his pockets it was everything he dreamed it would be. Farms offered only limited carnal delights, and besides he found himself with fellow sophisticates, witty, clever men and girls who knew how to have a good time, so he became the life and the banker of all events. Events – they have a manner of intervening unexpectedly, and so they did. He ran out of funds, likely sooner than later, and a famine ravaged the land. As Christ explained the youth's days of "riotous living" had passed and he was now bereft of so many things. His friends were gone, having vanished simultaneously with his money, homeless, hungry and most of all now totally lacking in pride or self—esteem. He, a Jew, born and bred, now took the lowliest most disreputable job that could be imagined. He became a feeder of swine, but even the pigs were better off than he for "...he would fain have filled his belly with the husks that the swine did not eat." It is so tempting to offer that the youth could not descend lower, but this is incorrect inasmuch as humans have an almost innate ability to sink deeper into a moral abyss. He did not, though, and Christ records that terse but meaningful phrase "He came to himself." Now, sitting in a filthy sty with the stench of swine assaulting his nostrils and his clothes stained by their effluvium "home" took on a different hue. It was now not the place of rules and restrictions, of arising in the morning to go to work and being surrounded by dull people, but rather it was the Edenic paradise where even the hired servants had enough bread "...and to spare." He now found true repentance when he examined his life and its options.

He is intelligent enough to know that one course only is left to him, and that is to return home; however, he knows that the return will not be as glorious as his departure, so he memorizes an introductory speech to deliver to his father:

> "and I will say unto him, Father, I have sinned
> against heaven, and before thee, And am no more
> worthy to be called they son: make me as one of
> they hired servants."

His journey home begins but travels not the entire route home. A long way from home his father espies him, runs to him, and in a moment of pathos collapses on the young man, kissing him and experiencing joy in its most unadulterated state this side of heaven. The son recites his spiel, but the father replies not with servitude but with honor and esteem. He is draped in a robe of fine fabric, the family signet ring placed on his finger and shoes on his feet. In the phrase that resounds yet today he directs the killing of the "fatted calf," and a party with music and dancing. For his son, once lost and dead is now found alive. The father had been in an abyss of his own, a pit of worry and grief over the state of his young son, and the unending worry, pain, self-persecution and self-doubt over his own character. What kind of father was I to allow this to occur he must have inquired of himself incessantly. In the twinkle of an eye all this now vanishes in view of the joyous homecoming. This is the time for celebration as no father could treat this an as ordinary day. Any father or mother in even the most remotely similar situation recognizes and more importantly feels the inexpressible elation of the father. Such is not exclusive to parents, for it is close to the same exhilaration felt when any who are meant to be together, then apart are reunited. Further, as intense as these emotions are in the parent-child relationship, neither fatherhood nor motherhood is a requisite to the experiencing of such intense happiness.

What a parable and what a story the Master has told. If this was the end of our narrative a great moral story it would remain to this day, and the Parable of the Prodigal Son would be taught as exemplary of the love and patience of God. We would marvel at the unsearchable depths of God's love and the grace He extends to the penitent believer, no matter the nature and course of his previous life and deeds.

But the Savior did not here end the story, and in point of fact has only told the half of it. To be a younger brother one must have an older sibling, and in this story it is an older brother who now makes his delayed entrance. Commendably he has been working in the field, and as he returns to his home he begins to hear the merriment and glee of festivities coming from the house. He stops short of the house and inquires of one of the family servants "what these things mean." The servant, undoubtedly over all that has transpired is glad to inform the elder brother that his younger brother has returned with the father proclaiming a celebration not only because of the return but also because he is now home "safe and sound."

The Bible is not a book of melodrama nor does it contain even a hint of self-dramatics. The scenes given to us speak for themselves, but we are permitted some leeway in commentary on the action and the dialogue. To say that the elder brother was underwhelmed by this rapid recitation of events and the quickly changed atmosphere of the home is an understatement of colossal proportions. Instead of being happy that his younger brother has come home Christ succinctly states that "he was angry and would not go in."

As is most often the case the father makes the next move, comes outside to see his son and literally begs him to enter and join the party. Effectively, though, the father has now given his elder son a stage upon which to air his grievances, obviously long held and perhaps even in some eerie way cherished by him. He opens with an introduction that is simultaneously self-serving and one of the most outrageous falsehoods to ever be uttered:

> "Lo, these many years do I serve thee, neither trans-
> gressed I at any time thy commandment."

On its face this is as patently absurd a statement as an individual anywhere and at any time could make. No mortal person could ever rightfully claim to never having done wrong in any relationship, especially one as long, emotional and intimate as father and son. Yet this son is not deterred from such an outrage. Even his wording reveals his special insight into his standing with his father, for he employs the word "commandment." Maybe a small child will see the parent-child relationship as command-obey, but a grown man such as the elder son should have put aside this thinking long ago. The text reflects that he is rendering service to a loving, gentle father, not a harsh authoritarian master. It reveals that the older son, while performing dutiful service and work, has always viewed his relationship with his father bathed in a harsh, legalistic glare. He simply does not or will not understand the goodness of his father.

Returning to his assertion or having "never" transgressed, this signifies a moral egoism and hubris that may be even more common than is thought but still is rarely expressed so starkly. This son has created for himself a moral stage on which he is the only player of consequence, and has a childish resentment when others are honored or even considered.

He continues to tear down his façade as the self-designated good son with a statement dripping in self-pity:

> "...Thou never gavest me a kid, that I might make
> merry with my friends."

Before we proceed with further comment may we not raise a query as to what sort of "friends" a man such as this would possess? In the event self-pity and sorrow is a locale all persons visit from time to time and it does not necessarily disclose or reveal fatal human weakness. What this remark discloses, though, is a spirit of false self-awareness and in the plainest of terms, a short memory. For however long the prodigality of the younger son was maintained for that same period the elder son retained a place of honor, position and esteem in the house of the father. While the younger brother writhed in the mud and filth of the pig sty the elder brother ate not with the servants but at the table of his father. His memory is somewhat selective as well, and for this we are reminded of Christ's construction of the narrative. When the younger son requested his inheritance, Jesus said, the father divided unto "them" the two brothers the estate. As noted by Jewish law and custom the elder brother had already been bestowed with twice the amount afforded to the younger. The elder's grief and petulance almost demands that we see this as an outburst of "What have you done for me lately?"

The elder son is still not finished with his father. As a viper sinks its fangs into its victim the son has venom to release when he again calls his father to task for celebrating the younger's return.

> "But as soon as this they son was come, which hath
> devoured thy living with harlots, thou hast killed for
> him the fatted calf."

Even the hired servant referred to the younger son as "your brother" but the elder son could only spit two words which became an epithet, "your son" not his brother. When these two words are read echoes of many millennia past resound as again we hear Cain's response to God regarding the whereabouts of younger brother Abel, "...Am I my brother's keeper?" Fathers and mothers note such as this and in a brief two-word phrase he has given plain insight as to what he really thinks of his father's younger son, and by implication the father himself. In unbrotherly fashion he assumes the very worst of his brother in that "...he has devoured thy living with harlots." Possibly, maybe even probably, this was true, but he had no evidence of such as assertion. His younger brother had been away in a far country, and as for himself, he had even refused to go into the house and see him. True brotherly feeling does not assume the worst of a brother.

Christ's most famous parable reaches its conclusion and we are left with a bittersweet taste. The father, ever gentle, ever loving, ever optimistic assures his son that he has not been shortchanged in fatherly love and affection, for "...thou art ever with me, and all that I have is thine." He defends his loving and even majestic greeting of his younger son by assuring the elder that the "dead" son was lost and "...now is alive" and "found."

Does there exist such an object as an accounting ledger for parents? Does a father keep a record of gains and losses among his children? Assuming that such a thing does exist, it is time to take the measure of this family. It will not and cannot serve as a final accounting for Christ left the remainder of the family's story untold. Yet at this juncture the status of the father and two sons begs for analysis and examination.

The younger son, invariably presented as the antagonist of the narrative, always has first claim on our disgust, anger and ultimately sympathy and happiness. He is, after all, the Prodigal Son. The natural first reaction to him, though, is one of revulsion and repugnance. The mature mind instantly grasps the foolishness and ingratitude of "demanding" an inheritance which he has not earned. Something else, though, do many minds in their maturity grasp as well, and that is some degree of identification with his arrogant demands. It is so natural for young men to wish to strike out on their own, establish their name and their independence. This is natural as breathing, but unfortunately the young, and especially young men, are great purveyors of ingratitude. This attitude seems to reach a type of pinnacle with the younger son. So off he goes, but the inheritance is not utilized for education or training, to buy a farm or a business, but is rather entirely consumed by the devouring hedonistic appetites of the son and his new found friends. When the crash comes so come other traits. The reality of life's harshness, the realization of his own stupidity and sin and the recognition that only the Father can provide what he needs. He has beaten down by life's frequent tremors and by his own folly but has begun to attain the one quality that is indispensable in God's eyes, humility. His pride led to his fall, and on his return home he arrives self-chastised and more than ready to mount the lowest rung on the ladder. He has abased himself, but in the words of Christ those that humble themselves will later be exalted. Satisfied to be a servant he comes home to sit at the table of the King, his own father.

In return to the Father could not have been made unless the Father was with the son in the beginning. Those portentous words of "He came to himself" reveal more than just a recognition of the trouble he had made for himself. To come to yourself implies that there exists some foundation, some moral structure that is always and ever present, regardless of the outward circumstances. That moral superstructure was provided by his father and in a very real way it was his father. Even at the nadir of degradation he knew that his father alone could be relied upon, and even here the younger son far underestimated the love and the strengths of that father. He was resigned to being a servant, but he had finally realized that in his father's house was an abundant supply of what the world did not provide "... and to spare." No doubt the young man's continued life was not an ever upward never interrupted arc into sunlit uplands, but for now he was home "...safe and sound." The father had gained a son.

For all the attention given the younger son these past two thousand years (and rightfully so) it is the older brother who provides a great breadth, depth and span of interest. Except when he relates an obvious falsehood he should be given the benefit of the doubt and his word taken as face value. As a son and a man, he evidently was a hard and faithful worker, and in fact his appearance in Jesus's parable finds him apparently coming home from work. Of course, we must discard his representation that he had never violated his father's commandments, for no person legitimately may aver such a proposition. He possessed an abiding respect for laws, rules and family proprieties and was likely very dependable in almost all things. Still, these were not the only qualities which he could call his own. A self-satisfaction and self-assurance of his own "flawless" life deeply marred his character. He effectively usurped the position of his own father when he declared to him that his own sterling and longstanding high moral character merited a special reward. His sense of moral self-assurance allowed him to condemn his younger brother's supposed (but unproven and even lacking evidence) dalliance with harlotry, while in the same moment ignoring his own haughtiness in judging his brother.

Unfortunately, the elder's bitterness towards his younger brother has historically clouded and even hidden a greater character disgrace that he owned, an even greater bitterness towards his father. Serious parents notice serious remarks, and the older son's acerbic flippancy in referring to "your son" rather than "my brother" undoubtedly had the sting of a scorpion to the father. We require no depth of this family's history to realize that he is consigning the real blame for the younger brother to the father. It is "your" son, and you bear the onus of his failure. It is so tempting to create a balance sheet for the father and state that on the day he gained one son he lost another. This may be so, but it is perhaps more likely that the elder son was not lost on this day but was already lost in his own self-satisfaction, self-sufficiency and bitterness.

To a father, though, the elder son's greatest sin occurred not in rejecting his younger brother but rather what he did to his father. On this joyous, festive, emotional day, maybe the greatest of his father's life, the older son casts a heavy blanket of darkness over every laugh, every note of music, every glad heart by his morose hateful attitude. The father's joy in the younger is now mortgaged to regret and worry for the elder. Perhaps Christ was thinking of the elder brother when He remarked of the scribes and Pharisees:

> "(T)hey honoreth me with their lips, but their heart
> is far from me."

In the historical record of the telling of this parable one character only has received the title billing, the younger son, always known as the lost son or more commonly, the prodigal son. Yet it is the father and alone the father that emerges as the central figure, the one truly indispensable person in the story. Throughout the ages and in all stories, fact, fiction, metaphorical, allegory, etc. it is almost impossible to find a character as consistent as is the father. With a singularity of attitude which rises to all demands and situations we see that his main attribute is the spirit of giving.

At the outset when the impatient young son demands an inheritance that is unearned the father gives it to him without acrimony or chastisement. When the prodigal returns from his self-generated and imposed period of moral and physical exile the father overwhelms him by giving up an undreamt of outpouring of love and forgiveness. He gives the young man a day of festivity where all join in the celebration of his unexpected return. While standing face-to-face with an older son, enraged and embittered, he gives understanding and consolation. The last act of giving perhaps is the most notable of all, for as he gives patience and tolerance he receives insolence and vitriol.

From the beginning to end the father is concerned most of all with reconciliation, a reconstruction of relationships as they were originally meant to be. He has found reconciliation with the younger son and his joyous attitude sparkles and glitters to all. The elder refuses reconciliation with his younger brother and reveals that he and his father were never really of the same heart and mind.

For all, though, the story still ends with hope. In the wake of receiving his older son's tirade he assures him that all he possesses belongs to him as well. The father gives and forgives, with home and hearth ever open and beckoning. What a father he was and remains forever, and yet we have only revealing, but slight glimpses into His true character. What awaits is eternity where His beloved apostle, John, promises "...we shall see Him as He is."

Chapter 13

LIKE FATHER, LIKE SON

*T*he plain truth is that so much of the character and personality of God the Father and His Son are beyond the ken and the understanding of mortals in this world. In the celestial, heavenly realm we are truly strangers and as Shakespeare once said it is "...the undiscovered country" from which none of us has returned. We still ponder and debate many of the same questions that were current throughout thousands of years of Biblical history. Scholars, historians, critics, theologians and ordinary persons still consider the greatest of questions, such as what is the origin of God Himself? If He has always existed, the "I Am That I Am," who or what is the force that brought Him into existence? More specifically and more importantly to this work if Jesus is His only begotten Son how did Jesus come into existence? By our lights and knowledge, all "begetting" requires a father and a mother, the latter character conspicuously absent from the Bible's narrative. All these questions and many more or great portent are worthy of discussion and study, but for all practical purposes the Bible has little concern for them. Its opening sentence simply and starkly proclaims His existence as a fact.

> "In the beginning God created
> the heaven and the earth."

For all the debates and studies throughout the centuries, all the books, sermons, societies, associations, creeds, dissertations, and on and on it really comes down to the believing Christian's acceptance of the Biblical story's inerrant truth or the disbelievers rejection of the story as nothing more than ancient mythology. The reasons for belief and the evidence for belief are endlessly varied. At this point in our work we must assume that to have continued reading, the reader must have some belief, and it is those we address our discussions.

For all our capacities and capabilities, we humans are incapable of grasping and really even intelligently discussing some of these issues. Is it possible that we can comprehend a Heaven or any type of world before ours? More pointedly may the heavenly and eternal relationship between the members of the Trinity, the Father, the Son and the Holy Spirit, really be understood? Dare we answer that question in the negative? Yet that answer itself begs a further question of whether we have real knowledge of the bonds and ties between them as they relate to our earthly existence? Generally, the answer to this query is yes, primarily because God has revealed these answers by declaration and example.

Perhaps the greatest lesson from the relationship between God and Christ which we may harvest is the true nature of perfection. It is a perfection wherein the concept contains a dual meaning. Our modern usage of "perfection" means flawless, without blemish, the realization of an ideal, and these are certainly true with the Father and Son. A longstanding traditional and historical meaning for the term focuses more on the idea of "completion," lacking nothing with everything possible having been done. To understand the perfection of Father and Son we are really called upon to view the relationship through the prism of Christ as a man, or more specifically the Son of Man. Jesus came to earth as God in human flesh and lived for thirty-three years as a man. He continually grew in stature, in wisdom and in favor with God and man. We can only speculate as to his days before the public ministry which commenced at age thirty, but he effectively succeeded in doing what we have been informed we cannot, that is serve two masters. He served His Heavenly Father and was a perfect and complete son to Joseph and Mary as well. Even before His public role began Jesus must have brought much pride to both His fathers. As He grew older He became aware that His special duality of character would at times lead to points in which he would have to choose one or the other. At age twelve, when accosted by His mother Mary in the temple He answered that He must be about His Father's business. He knew that with the progression of time He would leave His home and father in Nazareth to serve more fully His Heavenly Father; however, he never was remiss in any obligation to His parents. Even on the cross He made certain that His widowed mother Mary would be tended to by His close friend, the young apostle John.

As for His Heavenly Father, unlike most earthly parent-child relationships that between the Father and the Son always tended to veer in a straight line towards total, unbreakable unity. In the ministry of Christ, we find a remarkable consistency that for three years Jesus sought not His own glory and exultation but rather from beginning to end viewed Himself as the prime agent for His Father. His intention in the twelve-year-old teaching in the Temple has already been noted. His own views and His own emotions were often expressed but His Father's principality and reign over all was often noted. One day Jesus and His disciples came to the Temple to worship and to pray, but the sights, sounds and smells which greeted them there were hardly conducive to a frame of religious reference. As the Jews were required to present animals for sacrifice at Passover Christ was struck not only by the herds of oxen and sheep found there for that purpose, but also the moneychangers sitting in the temple haggling with customers over the exchange rate of Roman coins which had to be exchanged for Jewish currency, the only approved currency for temple offerings. Enraged by the mercenary nature of the scene and the desecration

James Kifer

of a holy place he made a whip of small knots and drove them from the temple. He lamented and exclaimed that they had turned "My Father's" house into a house of merchandise and a den of thieves.

When Jesus performed His endless series of miracles, the signs and wonders which so astonished the multitude, He was eager to give credit to His Father. Likely His most famous miracle through the centuries and certainly the one which garnered the most attention during His short lifetime was the resurrection of His close friend Lazarus, who had lain in his tomb for four days. For his sisters Mary and Martha, for the disciples and for the multitude to hear Jesus lifted up His eyes to heaven and said "Father, I thank thee that thou hast heard me," whereupon he summoned Lazarus from his grave.

The Savior seems to have special regard for His Father and the Father's love for Christ's disciples. Jesus saw and lived through a time that is the same as all times everywhere when He recognized that as a rule the sophisticates, the self-righteous and those smug from worldly wisdom rejected Him His exclamation was simply:

"I thank thee, O Father, Lord of heaven and earth,
because thou hast hid these things from the wise
and prudent, and hast revealed them unto babes."

Christ even credited His Father for His own disciples, and yet it was the presence of the Son, His teaching, His character that drew the multitudes and caused men to say as did the soldiers who came back empty handed from a mission to take Him that "...Never man spake like this man." Only Jesus comprehended the full strength, power, majesty and love of His own Father.

In the most pressured, chaotic and stressful moments that anyone in our world has ever endured Christ readily acknowledged not His own person or power, but that of His Father. On the Mount of Olives on the dark night before His crucifixion on Calvary the priests and rulers had brought hundreds of

› 142 ‹

soldiers to capture this "desperate" criminal, Jesus of Nazareth. As for Himself he willingly acceded to His arrest but remarked:

> "Thinkest thou that I cannot now pray to my Father,
> and He shall presently give me more than twelve
> legions of angels."

In such a moment of drama and ominous terror's lurking Christ readily remain linked to His Father's power. As the grim hours and minutes of the Passion proceeded apace, Jesus spoke little, but the few words He uttered again demonstrated His awareness that His Father controlled all. Before the mighty Pontius Pilate, the Roman governor, Jesus was literally face to face with a type still all too common in the world, the bully who has managed to gain and wield power. Pilate found himself in the tightest most excruciating bind in which any politician could find himself caught. He knew that this Jesus who stood before him was an innocent man, but he was also coping with a large blood fanged mob that sought His crucifixion. Above all as Roman governor he had to maintain Caesar's peace, and he was growing frustrated with this unusual man who stood before him, a man who seemed totally resigned to a horrible death and who rarely uttered a word. Finally, the impatient and scared Pilate menacingly threatened his prisoner and said:

> "Speakest thou not unto me? Knowest thou not that
> I have power to crucify thee, and have power to
> release thee?"

Jesus finally responded, but with words and in a manner to which a Roman governor was unaccustomed:

> "Thou couldest have no power at all against me,
> except it were given thee from above."

In a moment overloaded with drama, pathos, hatred and fear, the Son of Man automatically thought first of His Father and attributed to Him the real source of all authority.

Almost without end and from only four short gospels we may discover endless attributes of respect, love and even awe from the Son of God to God Himself. But what of the reverse, and especially in consideration of this small work's theme being that not of childhood but rather parenthood? It is a bit strange to even word this in any fashion but let us focus the lights of examination on the Father's relationship with His Son. Succinctly expressed, what did God as a parent think of His only Son, Jesus Christ?

A good father or mother is inclusive of their children, and by definition does not seek their exclusion from any good thing, and so it was with God. In the Bible's initial chapter and in its description of His most important act of creation He stated:

"Let us make man in our image, after our likeness..."

Much scholarly debate has arisen from these few words, but it is difficult not to view the consistent plurality of the pronouns "us" and "our", indicating that from the outset creation was a product of the Holy Trinity of the Father, Son and Holy Spirit. In the simplest of terms, the Son worked with the Father from the beginning and was a part of all manner of things. As was earlier alluded to we are at a severe handicap if not impossibility in trying to examine and discuss the Heavenly relationship with the Father and Son; however, this does not apply to earth.

Only the worst or most indifferent father would desire for his child a life of tumult, chaos and strife, but only God could make in Bethlehem of old such a birth announcement when His Son was born:

"...on earth peace, good will toward men."

Even Jesus's short life seemed to contradict God's declaration, but in reality, not so. Yes, Christ's life was filled with turmoil, personal attacks, vilification and a hideous death, but the peace Christ brought was humanity's reconciliation to His Father, a reconciliation that stands even today. God is the one and only father ever who could declare this. Then, for some thirty years God is recorded as having said little or nothing about His Son. One bright day when the prophet John the Baptist was preaching to the multitude he espied his cousin, Jesus of Nazareth, and dramatically proclaimed "Behold, the Lamb of God." Jesus had come to be baptized, and a reluctant John the Baptist complied. In the simple yet elegant words of the scriptures God has proclaimed both His love and His pleasure in a Son unlike any other, and that pleasure and pride was soon to be demonstrated anew.

Jesus apparently maintained an inner circle of three among His twelve apostles, three men with no more status or power that the others but likely had personal bonds and ties with Jesus greater than the other nine. These three were Peter, James and John, the latter two brothers. Shortly before His Passion Christ ascended a high mountain, and accompanying Him was this trio, who were now to behold an awesome sight and receive a foretaste of Heaven. Jesus was suddenly transfigured, and both His person and clothing became luminously bright and radiant; and He became host to two guests, perhaps the most revered figures in Old Testament history, Moses and Elijah. The ever expressive and ebullient Peter, doubtless with the best of intentions, exclaimed that there should be built three tabernacles to honor the three Jesus, Moses and Elijah. Peter's enthusiasm had led him beyond the boundary, though, and by implication such an act would have made the two men, great as they were, the equal to Christ, the Son of God. A bright cloud appeared, and a voice spoke familiar words, but likely in a tone different than heard at the baptism:

> "This is My beloved Son, in whom I \
> am well pleased, hear ye Him."

James Kifer

The apostles, shaking with fear, fell on their faces. Early in the scriptures humanity is informed that God is a jealous God and in fact the very first of The Ten Commandments resoundingly proclaims that "Thou shalt have no other gods before me." As the Father is jealous of His power and authority so is He with that of His Son's position and stature. In point of place Christ sits on God's right hand, and the Father quickly condemns any attempt, express or implied, to elevate man or beast to that level. In simple terms, the Father is always "looking out for His Son."

Parental love may also be expressed in anger, not anger at the child, but anger that can grow to cataclysmic proportions, towards any person who would harm or who has harmed our children. Our brief work is not engaged in a pure study of God's plan of redemption and of Christ's death, burial and resurrection; however, one key element of these events must be mentioned in any study of God's attitude towards His Son. On that Good Friday so long ago God witnessed the crucifixion of the only truly innocent person who ever lived, His Son Jesus Christ. He did not stop the proceedings, but His anger and wrath were awesome to behold. By noon God had darkened the entire earth with a blanket of black that lasted for three hours. He tore the veil of the Holy of Holies in the sacred Jewish temple from top to bottom, and earthquakes added to the fear of all mankind. His emotions, too deep and varied for humanity to fully comprehend, were at a minimum expressed in His anger that His beloved Son had to endure such a death for the redemption of a scornful, ungrateful humanity. Maybe for the first time since the days of Noah the Almighty truly, if but for a moment, regretted the creation of man.

Almost all sons wish to please their fathers, and at least when young wish to emulate their fathers in speech, fashion and action. Always a factor of detriment, but increasingly in modern society is the very real tragedy that untold numbers of sons are simply lacking any father, or any man whatsoever, on which to pattern their behavior and life itself. None of us, though, is lacking the exemplar of a Heavenly Father, and neither are we wanting in examples of professions of love between Father and Son. At the risk of repetition, it must again be said that we earthly mortals cannot really grasp the extent of the unity and unbreak ability of these bonds, for the relationship between God and Christ seemingly presents us with a logical (but not a Divine) impossibility. The Father and Son were both perfect, they were complete, and they have both always been extant. Their love for each other was perfect from the beginning, yet it is a love that was seemingly infused with continual growth. Although Christ sits on the right hand of the Father He stated, without hesitation, to His apostle that "I and my Father are one." Most of us have a loving relationship or fond memories of a father but even the closest may not proclaim that they are one. Christ could and did. So close was their being, their thinking, their love for one another and for humanity that Jesus could make such an astounding proclamation.

The statement is simple yet any question regarding the relationships in the Holy Trinity of Father, Son and Holy Spirit seems to be inherently complex. Even the men chosen by Christ to be apostles, men who worked and lived daily with Jesus for three years found the concept's grasp evasive. Near the end of His ministry the eager apostle requested of the Lord that he would be "satisfied" if Jesus just showed him the Father. An exasperated Christ was disappointed in Philip's lack of growth and simply responded:

"...(H)e that hath seen me hath seen the Father."

This, among countless other incidents, should put to rest the old ignorant belief of the wrathful God of the Old Testament and the caring, gentle, loving Son of the New Testament. The Father was wrathful and even vengeful when He needed to be, but never to His Son, and similarly never was Christ to His disciples. How often has all of Christendom needed the reminder given us by Matthew of the ancient prophet Isaiali's words:

> "He shall not strive, nor cry... A bruised reed shall
> He not break, and smoking flax shall He not
> quench."

Yes, the Savior could turn His wrath and one time even violence upon those who desecrated the temple, but His disciples were offered the succor and nourishment of plain, gentle, if sometimes sharp, words. The wrathful God, be He Father or Son, is not wrathful towards His own children, and in this as in all matters, the Father and Son are one.

Was it then and is it now even possible for the wills of the Father and Son to be different, to diverge and lead in different directions and results? Yes. On the night before His crucifixion, with sweat pouring off Him as if it were rivulets of blood in the deepest agony Christ prayed to His Father:

> "Father, if thou be willing, remove this cup from
> me: nevertheless, not my will, but thine be done."

If ever the duality of Jesus was shown in full panoply it is this moment. As a man of flesh and blood He feared and dreaded the pain, degradation and brutalization of death on the cross, but as a Divine Son His own will was that He subordinate Himself to the will of His Father. Thus, by this redemptive act the road to salvation was opened. To this day and forever the convergence and meshing of two wills, Father and Son, remains for all humanity as its ultimate example of the desirably close relationship between parent and child, an idealization that became reality with the Father and with Jesus.

In this life even the finest and most loving of parents and children may find themselves at cross purposes temporarily, but the bonds of real love never break. All of us have as the ideal the Father and Son of heaven and earth, although we know that in this life such an ideal will not be attained. Yet ever are we comforted by the ideal and by the closeness of God and Christ. In our understanding the mutual confidence and love they have for one another reaches its zenith on Judgment, for then will the most important of all actions for all eternity is entrusted to the Son, the judgment of every soul who has ever lived.

CONCLUSION

fter our brief journey through the Bible is it possible to draw relevant lessons from these few stories on parenthood? A brief glance could easily result in the conclusion that in the main they are episodic stories of family struggles, perhaps interesting and even illustrative but lacking any commonality. A deeper analysis, though, has no difficulty in locating several binding threads that weave through the fabric of the individual stories, threads that are recognizable in all parent child relationships. The easiest way to deduce the similarities of the stories and their characters is to sort them into categories. Ordinarily, this is a questionable strategy, for human beings and their characters do not always lend themselves to categorization; however, since a single aspect of life, parenthood, has been the main subject of concentration this approach seems to be reasonable.

Although many categories, sub-categories and arrangements are employable let us briefly review the parents we have observed as they are placed into five separate categories.

The first category would be those that are in modern terms the parental "role models", and they would include Mary and Joseph, Naomi, and Lois and Eunice, a diverse grouping indeed, spanning over one thousand years of Bible history. In some respects, a charge that these persons have little in common, but this will not withstand a more scrutinous eye. Likely, Naomi appears oddly placed for she is not even known as a mother but rather as a mother-in-law to Ruth.

Her lengthy trials and travails in life were such that no person would ever envy. She grew weary and embittered by grief, loss and disappointment, but her underlying character was so strong and so admirable that in her darkest moments she drew a pledge of lifetime devotion not from a daughter, but a daughter-in-law. Although the prime mover in pressing circumstances that would lead to the wedding of Ruth to Boaz she was always content to remain in the background. The background is the locale of Lois and Eunice, the grandmother and mother of Timothy, but their shadows spread throughout the early church and were writ large in the character of Timothy, one of our early Church fathers and at the end of Paul's life one of the great apostle's two or three closest confidantes. The spiritual descendants of these two women have loomed larger in history than perhaps anyone but God has ever realized. These mothers may remain essentially anonymous to all but the children they raise and to God, but their importance never abates. Two hitherto obscure young Nazarenes, Mary and Joseph are, of course, included in this grouping. Twenty centuries after their appearance they remain and deservedly so, the most recognized parental names in all of Christendom. Neither has any particular notoriety for a specific parental act, and they remain most recognizable as the earthly parents of the Messiah. An earlier chapter spoke to this and other facts of their lives. With Mary and Joseph in the fore of all parental recognition and plaudits what is most striking of this group of parents in their "normalcy", a word seldom employed today but once of popular currency. The lives of these persons are not of themselves spectacular and hardly the material of legends and glamour, but they continue to resonate from the present to eternity.

Many parents, perhaps even a majority of parents recognize those fathers and mothers of the Bible whose hearts and intentions are basically good but who are left with mixed and uneven results, and too often even heartbreak and tragedy. Neither then nor presently are all parents' perfect models to be emulated, but nonetheless even flawed, though basically good, mothers and fathers are those from whom we may learn an abundance. Those perused in this study would include Isaac and Rebekah, Jacob and his wives Leah and Rachel, and the priests and judges Eli and Samuel. A fair reading of their stories directs that we say that underlying favoritism, neglect and even treachery love for their children was to be found, even though it often lay dormant and undiscovered. Rebekah and Isaac were poisoned with favoritism, but each, especially Rebekah, knew the character of their sons and directed their parental actions guided by these understandings. Rebekah's end design for Jacob was correct, but the means she employed divided her family for a generation and almost destroyed it. All in the family suffered grievously for these errors, but none suffered more than the parents. The familial bonds, tenuous in the early days and stretched to the limited ultimately held in the end.

Jacob, the last of the three great patriarchs, repeated the mistakes of his parents, yet on a larger scale and stage. With polygamy the order of the day he added to the family mix multiple wives and mistresses and sired a total of thirteen children. His intense love for his youngest two sons was always evident, and thankfully the passage of years also revealed evidence of love for all his children. Yet his extreme favoritism towards Joseph ignited a series of events which altered the fate of nations and hastened the designs of God.

Later in the portraits of Eli and Samuel are truly painted the varying hues of travail and triumph. Eli was a conscientious man and priest and appeared fully attentive to his spiritual duties. Yet he today stands symbolically as the good man who for whatever reason, likely many, was not a good father. His grief and tears, though, were heartfelt and real when he learned of the deaths of his two opprobrious sons. Samuel, perhaps Israel's greatest judge, was a paragon and model of virtue and vitality and was as reliable as any man or woman found in the Bible's pages. His life was a song of obedience to God and he rarely failed Him. A man of great character, wisdom and judgment these traits were his alone for they were either not transmitted to or they were rejected by his corrupt sons. From creation forward how many fathers and mothers can sense a kinship with Samuel? The inability of children to share their parents' values and standards is an incessant source of strife, contention and even heartache. All in this category tried, likely some more than others, but while Isaac, Rebekah, Jacob, Eli and Samuel, may merit criticism they likewise should focus our understanding upon them. Parental mistakes are inevitable, but it remains a truth that the parent child relationship is both strong and elastic and so often can withstand almost anything so long as its foundation is love.

A third category may be drawn and explained so widely that is may include almost everyone. Among so many definitions parenthood is a series of experiences from which we either learn or remain ignorant. The Biblical record is host to an abundance of men and women very much like parents of any century and any culture in that they, especially fathers, really do not know what to do and what should their direction be when they assume these responsibilities. Judah, the fourth son of Jacob was an intelligent, generally responsible but a hard man who made a terrible blunder and sin, not with a daughter or son, but with his daughter-in-law Tamar. After knowingly engaging the services of a prostitute but ignorant of his incestuous relationship with Tamar, Judah's learning curve commenced its upward arc. He realized the baseness of his own behavior and learned from it, beginning a growth that would see him become the de facto leader of his brothers.

Unfortunately, much parental learning comes from suffering and all parents without exception have tasted of it. Hopefully many learn good and wise things, but yet not all. This brings our narrative to one final view of perhaps the most bewildering father in the Bible, David. As a man and a king, he displayed almost unmatched gifts, intelligence, creativity, and often great wisdom, but did he ever learn from his own fatherly mistakes. Likely it was a combination of inattention, neglect and perhaps disinterest, but David failed as a father. A man of intimidating brilliance his father son relationships often ended disastrously and even in death. David's ambitions and masculine desires always triumphed over fatherly responsibilities, and assuredly the sword never departed from his house.

Into a fourth category of parenthood we consign a short but strangely grouped list of parents, Saul, Herod Antipas and Herodias, a trio of names incongruously tied together. Our first impulse is to state that this woman and two men represent the outright parental failures. Yet with Saul, can any man who produced such a son as Jonathan be labeled a failure? Jonathan, a prince in fact and in deed, was the man that his father should have been. He was brave, steadfastly loyal and the very definition of friendship, while Saul proved to be weak, vacillating, cruel and vindictive. As a king Saul started well and bravely, but inherent moral weakness and insane jealousy of David ultimately destroyed him. His two most famous children, Jonathan and his daughter Michal became tools of manipulation for use against his enemies, real and imagined, especially David. It stretches reason and fairness to say any good of Saul as a father, a man who not once, but three times, attempted to kill his son Jonathan, a son who never betrayed his father and remained with him until death.

Herod and Herodias generally are considered outside the orbit of Biblical characters from whom we draw life's lessons, yet their story has demanded a forum in which to be heard. Sadly, the moral character of Herod Antipas and his wife, Herodias was little different than that possessed by multitudes of parents of any time and place. These two hideous manifestations of humanity obtained access to that most volatile of all commodities, power, especially when held in the clutches of immoral dregs such as these two. Herod was in every way a coward and Herodias could claim the heart of a murderer, and together they contaminated any situation and any person who crossed their paths. Herodias salivated over the prospect of the death of her detractor John the Baptist, and she was fortunate to possess not one, but two instruments to her ends, a stooge in her husband Herod, and the seductive charms of her nubile young daughter Salome. Few parents have ever descended to the depths of decadence found by Herod and Herodias. Neither has there been an abundance of fathers such as Saul, who used both son and daughter in his increasingly deranged attempts to destroy a presumed enemy. They stand as men and women who nonetheless merit a memorialization still today. Bad persons make bad mothers and fathers.

We are left with a fifth category and instead of "parents" it is the singular, yet two chapters, Twelve and Thirteen, have been devoted to its discussion. In the parable of the Grieving Father or the Lost Son it is easily discernible that this is an allegorical tale with the father of the two sons symbolizing the Heavenly Father. It is a short story in which much of God's character and personality is revealed, and the story alone should entice anyone to follow Christ, who has such a Father. This is a Father who gives and forgives on an almost infinitely abundant plane, who Himself absorbs shocks, griefs, worries and ingratitude and still looks for wayward children to return. The Heavenly Father's Son, though, has never supplied Him with shock, grief and certainly not ingratitude. The only begotten Son, Jesus, is totally at one with Him and has given God only pleasure, joy and love. The abiding story of the Father's love is secure in Christ, but just as certain in those that are His disciples.

How deep and unsearchable is the love and the riches of God, wrote the great apostle Paul. From the opening chapters of Genesis to the concluding pages of Revelation we discover an unending story of God's great abiding emotion of love for all His creation, but especially for its pinnacle, humanity, a humanity which for all its failures, its rise and its fall, is loved by the Father at a level no man or woman can truly comprehend. The believer instantly grasps and even senses that the Father's only begotten son, Jesus Christ, merits such parental love. Yet as wondrous as is this relationship between God and Christ a greater realization overwhelms the believer, for again as Paul declared:

> "...(W)e are the children of God: And if
> children, then heirs, heirs of God and
> joint-heirs with Christ."

Let us conclude with a remembrance of thousands of years past, in the days when Joseph had risen high in Pharaoh's favor, so high that Joseph was assured that "only in the throne" was Joseph not the equal of the king. An immensely grander throne is established in Heaven, and there sits the real king, Christ, on the right hand of His Father. Only in that majestic throne does He occupy a higher place with God. The greatest, most universal and most eternal of all truths, parental or otherwise, is that God loves all His children as much as He loves Christ.

CPSIA information can be obtained
at www.ICGtesting.com
Printed in the USA
FFHW010612291018
49004732-53269FF

9 781633 571624